An Entrepreneurial Leap

My Faith, My Lessons, My Success

Rachel Bickham

An Entrepreneurial Leap: My Faith, My Lessons, My Success

Printed in the United States of America

Paperback ISBN: 978-1-963732-00-9

Hardback: 978-1-963732-01-6

The Publishing Pad

www.thepublishingpad.com

Praise for an Entrepreneurial Leap

First, I would like to say this is a MUST-READ book of a woman who has overcome many obstacles in her life, both personally and professionally. What I really love about this book is the blind faith of her journey through lifelong lessons and how she was able to analyze, rebound, and dissect each situation to conquer her fears. Importantly, the highlight of the book is that the author inserted positive affirmations that not only built her to become the butterfly she has become today but also shed light on the path that led her to her success. I admire her courage and resilience in telling her story to help others. She is the epitome of a tenacious woman. Great job on your thoroughly accomplished debut, Rachel.

Phyllis Skipper, CEO
Estoria Transportation, LLC

An Entrepreneurial Leap: My Faith, My Lessons, My Success is a must-read for anyone who aspires to be a successful entrepreneur. Rachel's story is a powerful testament to the vulnerability, tenacity, and perseverance required to start, build, and run a thriving business. This book provides valuable insights and lessons that every entrepreneur needs to succeed in their journey. The affirmations at the end of each chapter are a bonus, providing a powerful mindset shift during tough times. Whether you are just starting or have been in business for years, *An Entrepreneurial Leap* is a valuable resource that can help you achieve your goals and overcome any obstacle.

Shanita Johnson, PMP, CSM
President, BKJ Global Management Consulting, LLC
www.bkjgmc.com

An inspiring account of the author's journey to becoming a successful entrepreneur, Rachel Bickham shares how, through her mistakes and triumphs, she remained faithful to God and landed on some very insightful lessons every entrepreneur should know.

Using her experience as a seasoned entrepreneur as a guide, Bickham provides an incredibly valuable roadmap for successfully navigating the challenges and pitfalls of entrepreneurship, offering practical, battle-tested solutions that will promote success in your business.

A powerful resource for aspiring and current entrepreneurs alike.

Deshonda P. Charles, Esq.
CEO | Attorney at Law
D. Charles Law Firm, PLLC
www.DcharlesLaw.com

What was most impressive about this book is how Rachel allows the readers to gain access to the source of her struggles with faith. Rachel shared some of her childhood trauma and how it affected her self-esteem and self-worth. As an African American female, we tend to think discrimination is something that can be found outside of the home. However, colorism among family members is something we rarely hear and talk about. Being a woman of faith, Rachel shares how she had to trust in God, but also how she was able to utilize tools and coping strategies to unlearn self-sabotaging behavior. Often, we are told to just pray and wait. However, Rachel shares the steps it took to heal mentally and spiritually.

This book is an excellent guide to entrepreneurship. However, as a therapist, this book is an excellent guide to help those along their healing journey.

Thank you, Rachel, for allowing us to share in your journey and giving us tools to aid in our own.

Larneka Lavalais LPC-S
Larneka Lavalais, LPC PLLC
www.lavalaislpc.com

If there is one book that raises the bar, sweeping through the realms of empowerment, resilience, and enlightened action, it's *An Entrepreneurial Leap: My Faith, My Lessons, My Success*! It's a game-changing guide that inspires us at HJ Staffing as it mirrors our ethos. Breathe in the potent blend of her wisdom, reinforcing the potent empowerment we strive to provide to every job seeker and employer we serve.

Rachel's volume initiates an enlightening journey, bridging her staunch faith with fundamental techniques for traversing life's changing landscapes as an entrepreneur. Central to her thought-provoking guide is the experiential reality of divine timing, parallel to our belief in time aligning perfectly to fit the unique journeys of our candidates and clients.

Rachel's *An Entrepreneurial Leap: My Faith, My Lessons, My Success* is a compelling must-read. Get ready for self-discovery, for tapping into your potential, and for growing in ways you've never imagined.

Constance Jones
President & CEO of HJ Staffing
www.hjstaffing.com

Everyone has a story. Some stories reflect more challenges than others. In *An Entrepreneurial Leap: My Faith, My Lessons, My Success*, author and business owner Rachel Bickham gently weaves her personal and professional stories of trials, tribulations, and triumphs throughout the chapters to assist those traveling the rugged uphill journey of transformation to acquire key tools she previously lacked prior to her "Hard Knocks University" education.

Sharing valuable lessons acquired over the years, Rachel not only helps pave the entrepreneur and stakeholder's road with "gold nuggets" to navigate the tough terrain, but also provides a roadmap for a much smoother path to success. *An Entrepreneurial Leap: My Faith, My Lessons, My Success* is a must-read, whether you own a business or not.

Warren Winston, AMFB
Doing Business Unusual[SM]
www.winstonworldwide.com

Contents

Acknowledgements

First and foremost, I honor and thank God, who strengthens and guides me daily. Who set me on my entrepreneurial journey to learn and inspire others. This book would not exist without Him ordering my steps.

To the entrepreneurs I've learned from along my journey, who have given me invaluable insight and support, thank you: Phyllis Skipper, Constance Jones, Warren Winston, Moses and Cassandra Iku, Paula Howell, and others.

I want to express my love and deep appreciation to my late sister, Bridget Bickham, who instilled a strong work ethic and always encouraged me to be the best version of myself. She always told me I could do anything I put my mind to and not doubt myself.

I want to acknowledge my son, Darren R. Gardner, humbly. He's the reason why I keep going. I want to let him see that anything is possible when you trust and believe in God and yourself.

I want to express my love and appreciation to my family and friends who supported me from the start: My parents, Jessie Cousain and Ernest Bickham Sr.; my siblings, Earnest Bickham III (my twin), Carrie Bickham, Charlotte West, Phyllis Skipper, Friends; Ida MaBon, Christina Avila, JP and Erica Dada, Yesenia White, Victor and Leslie Seaborn, Michelle Fuentes, Larneka Lavalais, Wakeena Sweat, Dr. Sabeeta Singh, Warren Winston, Deshonda Charles, Shanita Johnson, Jonette Nagra, Shenill Johnson, and a host of others who provided support in many forms during my entrepreneurial journey.

Introduction

I have a story to tell. My story. It is a story of trials and tribulations, of taking leaps of faith. It's a story about resilience amid adversity, about triumph over defeat. My story isn't pretty or neat. It's messy, with some self-destruction, self-hate, self-sabotage, and growing pains—from healed to broken, broken to healed, and healed to broken again, a vicious cycle of jumping on and off hamster wheels. It's my truth about the lessons I've learned on my road to success.

I wrote this book hoping to inspire someone while telling about the things I've been through since I started my business. I want to share some of the hardest lessons I've learned: lessons of trust, failure, and self-love. I also want to support others who are just starting their business journey or may be struggling with tips to help them reach their desired height.

This book is not just a narrative; it's a tool kit for anyone who dares to dream and is brave enough to pursue those dreams despite the hurdles.

As you turn these pages, you will journey with me through the winding paths I have traversed in my career. You will experience my highs, my lows, and the in-betweens; the moments of stark clarity and the periods of over-whelming doubt.

But this is more than just my story. It's a mirror into the soul of every aspiring entrepreneur. It's a testament to the enduring spirit of anyone who has ever stood at the precipice of change, hesitant yet hopeful. In sharing my story, I want to light a path for you. This path is lined with practical advice, hard-earned wisdom, and the gentle reassurance that you are not alone in your journey.

The entrepreneurial journey is a complex one filled with twists and turns, challenges and rewards. It tests your resolve and shapes your character. In these pages, you will find my own experience, tests, and triumphs. I talk about trust, not just in others but in oneself; failure, not as an end but as a vital, often unavoidable step towards success; and self-love, the cornerstone of any true and lasting achievement.

At the end of each chapter, you will find powerful affirmations that will inspire you and support you through your life journey. Commit to embracing these affirmations, and they will transform your outlook, your approach, and perhaps even your life's journey.

As you embark on this journey with me, remember that every chapter you read is a step forward in your own journey. Every affirmation is a tool for your personal and professional development.

Let's explore the terrain of entrepreneurship together, learn from my missteps, celebrate the victories, and build a foundation for your own success.

Welcome to my story, a narrative woven from the threads of persistence, resilience, and unwavering determination. Let it be your guide, your motivation, and your inspiration as you navigate the exhilarating, challenging, and ultimately rewarding path of creating and growing your own business. Welcome to a journey of transformation, from the first step taken in fear to the pinnacle of entrepreneurial achievement. Let's begin.

CHAPTER 1

When God Says Go

LESSON NO. 1:

Don't neglect the feelings you're getting that it may be time to move in a new direction. Step out of your comfort zone and trust that God is telling you to go for a reason. Have faith and trust in His plan for your life.

In the last few years of my time working in corporate, I felt a nudge to move. There was something telling me that my time working in corporate was up. It was time for me to move on to the next chapter of my life. Have you ever been listening to the radio and a song played that aligned with what you were thinking or feeling? And then you got to where you were going and there was a sign that said what you were thinking or feeling? Well, that was happening to me just about every day. I kept getting signs that it was time to step out in faith and do what I had prepared to do. My business was already established as an LLC. I had obtained my minority certifications and was networking with government agencies. But I had no contracts yet and wasn't officially doing any business in Texas. I was still learning about staffing and failing miserably. I quickly realized that owning a staffing and recruiting business is more than just finding someone to do a job.

At the time, I was working in the oil and gas industry for one of the largest pipeline infrastructure companies. It was a good company to work for. The benefits were great, and my boss was awesome. My coworkers kept me entertained so most days went by fast. I couldn't believe what God was asking me to do: leave the stability I'd had for the past four years and step into something that I wasn't an expert at yet and knew little about. At one point, I thought I was losing my mind. I thought to myself, *Surely God isn't telling me just to quit my job when I have no safety net.* But that's precisely what he was telling me to do. To take a leap of faith. Trust that He would take care of me as He always had.

Prior to going into full business operations, I went to a meeting with two government agencies to present a draft staffing presentation. Each agency asked questions that the owner of a proper staffing company would and should know, but I didn't have the answers to any of them. I was ill-prepared. I felt embarrassed and uneducated about the industry I desperately wanted to be in. Rather than sulking or wallowing in self-pity, I went home that day and researched every question they asked. I researched my competitors, learned staffing terminology, and found out how to write staffing proposals. I obviously didn't know what I was doing although I was sure I wanted to do business with government agencies—just going off my passion and desire to help people provide for their families. So, when God told me to move when I didn't have any contracts yet, I was scared. I was confused. I questioned Him numerous times but kept getting the same answer until I could no longer deny what He was calling me to do. It was time to go. So, I told myself I was going to do it. If God said it was time to go, then it was time to go.

I wrote my letter of resignation and brought it to the office the next day. I was still nervous, but overall I felt a sense of peace knowing that God was with me. It was about mid-morning when I decided I was going to turn it in. Before I could get out of my seat, I received a text message from my son saying that he had just turned in his resignation from his job. That took me completely by surprise. We hadn't talked about quitting our jobs. I hadn't told anyone I was quitting, not even my son. I thought to myself, *How could we be thinking the same thing?* Then I asked my son if he had anything else lined up yet. He said no, he didn't have anything yet, but he felt like it was time to go and that God was going to make a way for him. Chills came all over my body at that moment. I couldn't believe it. His response to my next question almost made me drop the phone. I asked, "When is your last day?" He wrote back, "September 7th." I gasped! The date he gave his employer was the same date as mine. We were both giving a one-month notice on the same day with the same resignation date, and we hadn't discussed it. At that moment, I knew for sure I was doing what God had called me to do. I didn't have to question it anymore.

I got up from my chair to give my resignation but found that my boss wasn't in her office. She'd taken the day off. Therefore, I would have to wait until she was back. After work, I left the office and went home feeling a bit anxious. I had been so ready that morning, but by evening, fear began to creep in again. I began wondering what my boss was going to say when she found out I was leaving. I even questioned again if I was doing the right thing. Yet again, I heard a voice inside me saying, "It's time to go." So, I picked up my phone and texted my boss, letting her know I was turning in my resignation. She was shocked and wrote back, asking to speak with me before she accepted my resignation. She asked if I could hold off giving notice until she was back in the office. I agreed.

When she came back to work, I went to her office, still a little nervous, and handed her my letter of resignation. She was disappointed and didn't want me to leave without doing what she could to get me to stay. She called the director and the vice president of our department to see if there was anything they could offer. After a week of back and forth with the three of them, I declined all offers. I greatly appreciated their efforts, but I was convinced that it was time for me to go. She was sad to hear that I had decided to leave. She had been so good to me the two years I was in her department. I felt bad for leaving but also relieved. She asked if I could give them an extra week, pushing my date to September 14th, to find someone else, and I said yes. After all she'd done for me, that was the least I could do for her. Besides, it wasn't like I had anything else to do. She also offered me the option to remain with the company until I found something else. However, I still sorrowfully declined. I had to go. Nothing they offered was better than my stepping out on my own and following the path God laid out for me.

The month that followed was emotional. I knew I was leaving my team and would miss talking to them. It was also emotional because I was scared as to what my next steps were going to be. I had no clue how I was going to land a contract. I didn't even have a contract agreement written up at the time. I felt as if I were closing my eyes, spreading my wings, and jumping off a cliff hoping I wouldn't die. At the same time, I was happy, feeling liberated, and optimistic. If there is such a thing as happy fear, that's what I was feeling. I was ready for the next chapter in my life. I was trusting and believing that God would catch me and wouldn't allow me to fall. Therefore, I jumped with my arms wide open—and God caught me!

So, lesson number one is for you to move when God says go! Things may not be perfect, but when he says go, rest assured that he will make provision. All he needs from you is total obedience and trust that he's got your back and will see you through. When God says yes, he sets things in motion for your success. This doesn't mean that everything will begin to work out from the get-go. However, if you trust fully in him, he will direct your steps, provide what you need in every season, and lead you to people who are essential for your life's journey.

But how do you know when God says go? This depends on your relationship with God. God speaks to each of us differently. It could be a prompting in your heart, a strong feeling that there is something you should be doing. It could be through repeated dreams, or even hearing God clearly. God also uses other things and people to speak to us. The signs on the road, the words in a newsletter, the ad that suddenly shows up on your phone, even the words in this book. God will speak repeatedly and lay a burden in your heart to nudge you towards his will for your life. Often, when God speaks, He sends confirmation so that you are clear that He is the one speaking. I heard Him tell me it was time, and then I received confirmation from different sources, including the text conversation with my son.

Hearing from God is one thing, but having the courage to move is another thing entirely. That we know it's God speaking does not always remove the fear that comes with the unknown, and this is totally normal. It is okay to be afraid of what is out there, especially when you have a seemingly perfect present.

I get it. Even when we are sure that it is time for us to step out, we have to battle with the fear that we may not have heard correctly. But we must not let fear stop us from moving. In Joyce Meyer's words, "Fear will try to keep you from taking that first step. Don't give in to fear; do it afraid." Fear is a natural emotion that happens to almost everyone, if not everyone. The only differentiating factor is how we respond to fear. We can either allow fear to keep us grounded or use it as a stepping stone to the next season of our lives.

So how do we respond to the call to move to our next season in the presence of fear? Here are nine practical tips that will help you:

1. Acknowledge the emotion. Fear is our body's response to the unknown. We feel afraid when we are about to step into a new season, which is totally normal. The first step to overcoming this emotion is to acknowledge its presence. You need to realize that fear is not a sign of weakness but confirmation of the great journey ahead of you. Take a minute to acknowledge that you are afraid of the next step. This declaration is a crucial part of your self-awareness. When you are self-aware, you are able to address the cause of the issue. Acknowledging that you are afraid of the next season helps you seek to understand the reason for the emotion and allows you to confront it with a sense of purpose and clarity. Fear is not evil. Don't run from it. Rather, embrace it as a sign that what is ahead of you is very powerful.

2. Remind yourself that this is not your timing but God's timing. You have to trust in God's timing. God has confirmed that it is time for you to enter a new season in your life, and He is never wrong, even if it seems like your current season is the perfect one. I had a good job, and I didn't understand why God wanted me to move, but I trusted his divine timing. If he said it was time, I had to trust that it was time! Trust that God has a greater purpose for you and that He will reveal his plans for you with purpose and precision. Do not depend on your human understanding, but rather look to God for direction. Trusting in God's divine timing requires a shift in perspective—you must be willing to view the season as one controlled by God and surrender to Him totally. As you surrender to God's timing, fear begins to lose its grip, making it possible for faith to grow.

3. Think about past seasons of your life and the lessons from each season. Reflect on the strength, resilience and growth that accompanied those seasons. Recount times in the past when you embraced the unknown and came out a better person, with learnings and growth. Let these reflections serve as your reminder that you will win again in this new

season. Reflecting on past seasons helps you realize your capacity to adapt and thrive in new seasons. The challenges you overcame, the lessons you learned, and the growth you experienced during the process are signs of your resilience. Remembering all the things you overcame in the past and knowing that you are still standing will help boost your confidence to move on. See each season as a building block, creating the foundation of strength that you can stand on as you grow in your life's journey.

4. Ground yourself in faith. Engage in spiritual activities that will strengthen you and increase your faith, whether it be connecting with your faith community, praying, or meditating. Faith doesn't make the fear go away, but it gives you the courage to keep moving despite the presence of fear. Faith is knowing and trusting that even though the situation may not make sense right now, it will end in your favor. Faith is trusting that the divine has better plans for you and being dedicated to playing your part to ensure that you get to the new season God has created for you. You see, God has great plans for us, but He needs us to move towards His plan. Faith is what gives speed to our feet when our hearts are filled with doubt. Think about the times you stepped out in faith and how God showed up for you. Let that be the testimony that strengthens your heart to take another leap in faith despite the presence of fear. I trusted God's plan for my life, and now I'm able to share my testimony to help others.

5. Seek support and guidance. Have you found that your worries are reduced when you share them with the right people? It is the same with fear. As you share your fear with the right people, the fear is reduced. Seek counseling from your spiritual mentors, family members, friends, and those who have walked similar paths. Find a community of people who are starting a similar journey, and hold each other's hands. Thankfully, social media has made it easy to find a community of people with similar journeys and values. Share your aspirations and fears, and let these people support you on this new journey. Remember that different people are in your life for different reasons. Ensure that you are speaking with people who are better suited to help you with each problem. Sometimes you need the right person to help you make the

best decision, just like the texts from my son helped me conclude that it was indeed God telling me to make a change. Surrounding yourself with people who support and care for you will shelter you as you navigate the unknown. Hearing others share their experiences with difficult situations that helped them grow will encourage you and give you the boost to move on.

6. Break the milestones into manageable steps. Thinking of the big picture can be very fearful, I agree. However, if you break the goals into manageable steps, they become lighter and easier to manage. Define the big picture, then list the steps to achieving this bigger goal. Have a plan of all the things that need to be done and begin to prioritize them. Maybe you want to get some tools in place before you resign. Break the journey down into steps, and as you complete and check each item off your list, the victories become a testament to your resilience and courage, helping to dissolve fears. Consider the journey as a series of small, intentional steps, always putting one foot in front of the other. Every step is a triumph, a victory over fear, and a conscious choice to keep moving towards the new season. This helps manage the change in a way that reduces the fear and allows you to savor the increasing successes.

7. Cultivate a positive mindset. While it is easier to focus on what could go wrong, practice channeling your thoughts towards what could go right. Shift your mind from dwelling on the dangers to embracing the opportunities in the new season. Think of the great things you can achieve in this season. Think of the people you will help, the impact you will make, and every other positive result that could come out in this new season. Think about the blessing and the potential for growth that accompany this season. When you focus on the positive, you create anticipation and subdue fear. Remember that having a positive mindset does not mean that you are denying there will be challenges. It means that you choose to see these challenges as stepping stones rather than stumbling blocks. It's about acknowledging that every challenge comes with opportunities for transformation and growth. After all, you won't know what is on the other side if you don't move. As you focus on the opportunities that exist in this new realm, you begin to create an environment that encourages optimism and resilience, creating a way for a smoother transition into

your new season.

8. Celebrate your wins. As you make progress in this new season, take time to celebrate every single achievement, big and small. Record them in a journal, and refer to the journal each time fear creeps up. Recording your wins is a great way to motivate yourself to take the right steps in the presence of fear.

9. Practice gratitude. Often, when we move our attention from what we do not have to what we have, we experience a feeling of peace and assurance that comes only from gratitude. Gratitude helps to eliminate fear. It helps you realize your life's blessings and approach the season with positive anticipation. Express gratitude for the end of one season and the start of another. Express gratitude for the relationships, lessons, and experiences that have shaped you in past and current seasons of your life. As you do so, you open your heart to the numerous blessings and opportunities that await you in the new season. As you practice gratitude, you begin to let go of fear, replacing it with a deep sense of contentment and trust in the journey ahead.

When God says it is time for you to move into a new season, it is your invitation to step into the light of a new dawn. Embrace the journey ahead with an open heart and total trust that God will guide you to the end. Remind yourself that the new season holds so many promises that can only be achieved if you take the first step. Do it afraid!

Here are some affirmations for you to declare over your life daily:

★   I have a clear and defined vision for my life.

★   I am more resilient than I believe I am.

★   I am purposeful and deliberate.

★   I am intelligent and capable.

★   I am adaptable and open to change.

★   I embrace challenges and overcome them.

★   I always bounce back from setbacks.

★   I know my true purpose in life.

★   I am connected to my true calling.

★   I fully embrace the journey of life.

★   I actively seek joy and happiness.

★   I have complete confidence in my ability to create a life I adore.

★   I am living proof that dreams can become a reality.

★   My story serves as an inspiration to others, and it will continue to do so.

★   I refuse to let life bring me down.

★   I have no room in my heart or mind for doubt or negativity.

★   I choose to speak life into my dreams.

- ★ I choose to speak life into my vision.

- ★ I have faith in the process and timing of my life.

- ★ I believe my story will surpass my wildest imagination, becoming more prominent, better, and more beautiful than I could have ever dreamed.

CHAPTER 2

Doing All the Right Things Right

LESSON NO. 2:

Be prepared to go after what you want. That includes doing research, maintaining a tight budget, planning, and removing distractions.

September 14th had finally come—my last day of working for Corporate America. I really didn't have much work during my last week. All my job responsibilities had been transferred to my coworkers. I was coasting through the day when it finally hit me: I wouldn't have a steady paycheck anymore. Medical benefits would end in thirty days, and I would be solely responsible for every paycheck from now on. It was sink or swim time. I had to figure out how I was going to support myself quickly, so I thought. I felt intense stress as I wondered how I was going to conduct business development, make time to recruit, run daily operations, manage payroll, and do everything else needed to run a staffing company. I was so green to the industry, but I refused to let the lack of knowledge get me down. I was determined to figure it out. There were people who were unemployed, and I wanted to help them find jobs. There was no time for loafing. So, I prayed and asked God to send someone to help me.

Days later, I ran into a neighbor in the elevator lobby of my apartment complex. We had a brief conversation, and I reluctantly asked what she did for a living. To my surprise, she was a contract recruiter! Just what I needed. I asked if I could call her if I needed help with filling positions, as I had recently started a staffing and recruiting business. I was grateful she said yes! God had sent me whom I needed when I needed them. I was relieved! I began to focus more on business development now that I had someone on my team to assist.

After two weeks of being unemployed, I landed my first contract. I had gone to a networking event where I met a woman who needed my services for her spa company. She needed a front desk clerk to help her part-time. My first attempt to source someone for the position was an epic failure. The young lady I had scheduled for the position never showed up and didn't call on her start date. Once again, I felt embarrassed. I thought to myself, "It's my first contract and I couldn't even fulfill it correctly." I had already begun doubting myself and my capabilities. I didn't give myself any grace; I sought perfection from the start. It was classic self-sabotaging behavior. I reached out to my neighbor, and thankfully, she was able to quickly find someone with whom the client was happy.

My second contract came from another networking event I attended at a minority certifying council. One of the keynote speakers invited me to speak to a class of construction contractors. A student in the class took my card and contacted me the next day. I was elated! I got two contracts and filled them with my first two employees.

I was on cloud nine until I realized I had done all the right things wrong. Although I managed to secure the contracts, I realized my business expenses had been greater than my revenue. The cost of running my business didn't allow for any profit. For example, I had obtained the services of a payroll company before I had the capital to sustain the service. I had obtained workers' comp insurance only to realize Texas didn't require it for what I was doing at the time. In these and other ways, I was spending money unnecessarily as a startup company. I'd failed to take the proper time to plan the details of how to achieve my goals. I had a business plan, but I didn't follow it at all. I treated the business as a sprint and not a marathon. I was steamrolling ahead, making all kinds of mistakes.

Prior to quitting my job, I was bootstrapping my business, meaning I was paying for everything out of my own savings rather than with loans or investment capital. I had the infrastructure all set up before my departure, including my Applicant Tracking System (ATS), time tracker as well as the aforementioned payroll system and insurance. I saved a little up but not enough to sustain me for six months if I didn't get any contracts. Thankfully I was able to tap into my 401(k), IRA, and pension. But it wasn't just a tap; I withdrew every cent of it. I used the money for my personal bills as well as my business expenses. It seemed like the right thing to do at the time and given the circumstances. However, there I was again, doing all the right things wrong. Instead of cutting back on expenses and seeking mentorship on how to reduce startup costs, I continued doing business as usual. The struggle to maintain a healthy cash flow for both business and personal expenses was real.

A couple of months after starting my new business venture, I entered a new relationship. I was taking lavish trips and spending unnecessary money all in the name of freedom from corporate life. Although vacationing and having love in my life were what I thought I needed while starting up my business, that couldn't have been farther from reality. I was so focused on trying to be a good partner, helping my partner to heal old wounds that I didn't create, and trying to live my best life with my newfound freedom that I neglected my vision and purpose. I allowed those other things to distract me from focusing on building a solid foundation for the business. Of course, I can say that I had a little success here and there, but the truth is I allowed distractions to take me off task and hinder me from developing my full potential as a business owner. Being a good partner is important, no doubt. However, as an entrepreneur, my primary focus should have been on creating and ensuring the success of my startup company—especially since I was no longer receiving a steady paycheck.

Relationships can be distracting for entrepreneurs if they aren't balanced and there are no healthy boundaries in place. It took me a while to set healthy boundaries that were firm. Taking mental health breaks is essential, but instead of vacationing every chance I got, turning up with my friends every other weekend and during the week, I should have been using my downtime to study, research, and master my craft in order to show my commitment and passion for what I was doing and why I was doing it. I allowed my worldly desires to take me off my course. My newfound freedom distracted me from trudging forward with the plan God had placed me on. I was doing everything right—being a good partner, a good friend, and an inspiration to others. Yet I was doing everything wrong by neglecting my core needs and those of my business.

Those things were just the start of my distractions which led me to realize that I had not set healthy boundaries between myself and the people in my life. There were at least five businesses to which I gave away free business services, whether it was business consulting, administrative support, operations support, proposal writing, or attending meetings. Instead of giving away free services and knowledge, I could have invested that time in my own business and gotten paid for my talents. At the time, I thought I was doing the right thing, helping companies that would, in turn, help me. Boy, was I wrong. Each time, I ended up on a rollercoaster, running around in circles or in the middle of drama. None of these efforts proved to be lucrative to my business, and I ended up spending more money and wasting more time on other people's business ventures. I have no regrets because I do enjoy helping other small businesses succeed. But I should have requested compensation for my expertise and time. I should have done a better job of realizing my worth and value. I did all the right things wrong because I failed to put myself and my business first. So here are some tips to avoid certain pitfalls during the startup of your business:

1. The first few periods after you take off may be hard, but do not give up. Remain consistent. Use this time to master your craft. Seek knowledge. Network with experts in your field. Find accountability partners. Do everything you can to become a master of your skills. Be prudent with your spending. Create a budget and stick to it. Take time to review your expenses and take out anything that is not a necessity. While dining out and entertainment are good, they may not be the best decisions for you at the beginning of your next season. There are several ways to cut down expenses while you grow your business. If you are renting, consider moving to lower-cost housing. Have a shopping list and stick to the list when you go into the store. Buy only items you will use within the next week or two to avoid waste. Look for deals and shop with coupons. Make your meals at home. Look for cheaper, even free, ways to spend time with your friends and family. Review your entertainment subscriptions and cancel the ones you do not need. Entertainment is good, but let's be honest, how often do you have the time to watch Netflix and other subscription apps? Remember that this is only temporary, and you want to have enough funds to sustain yourself while you grow your business.

2. Set clear intentions. Before you start a task, ask yourself what you intend to accomplish from that task. What is the purpose behind your actions? What principles and values do you aim to uphold? When you set clear intentions, you are able to align your actions with your goals and values, ensuring that you are not merely moving but moving in the right direction. Setting clear intentions also helps you eliminate actions that are not driving you towards your end goal, even if they may be good actions.

3. Conduct proper research. Research everything related to the business you are going into. I obtained workers' comp insurance only to realize Texas didn't require it for what I was doing at the time. I could have avoided this cost if I had done my research. Proper research will save you time and money.

4. Have a detailed business plan. A business plan is your strategic vision, guide, and road map all rolled into one. It introduces your business, identifies the problem your business will solve, and explains why the business will succeed. It shows where you are going and how you will get there. Your business plan helps you to stay on track. Avoid distractions, no matter how enticing they may be. Allow room for flexibility, as things may happen that may require you to tweak your plans, but always keep in mind the overall goal for starting this new season in the first place. Refer to the business plan at intervals for motivation and inspiration.

5. Balance effectiveness and efficiency. Efficiency ensures that tasks are completed with the best use of resources, while effectiveness ensures that these tasks align with your main goal. Do not sacrifice one for the other, but rather ensure a balance between the two. Remember that the goal is not just to get things done but to do the right things in the right way.

6. Grow your knowledge and expertise. Take advantage of digital learning platforms, such as Udemy and Coursera, to sharpen your skills. Most of these platforms offer discounts and sometimes free resources to help you perfect your skills. There is also plenty of free content out

there to help you start and grow your business. YouTube, for example, is a great resource for any and every kind of learning, and you do not need a YouTube subscription to learn! I watched numerous videos on YouTube on how to run a staffing business. Reach out to experts and ask for mentorship opportunities. Today, you can reach out to people on LinkedIn and ask for guidance as you grow in your selected field. Find people who have mastered your craft and learn from them. Investing in continuous learning is one of the best gifts you can give to yourself.

7. Create healthy boundaries. Sometimes friends and family members want us to provide services to them at no cost simply because they are our friends and family. You must remember to create healthy boundaries and keep business separate from friendship and family. Businesses thrive when friends and family provide support. You may also meet others who are there only to take without reciprocating. Setting healthy boundaries will help you place things in perspective and treat your business the right way. This also includes your romantic relationships. Ensure that your romantic relationship doesn't distract you from pursuing and achieving your business and life goals. Setting the necessary boundaries will give you the time and space for creativity and help you thrive in your next level.

8. Give yourself grace. Know that you may make mistakes. Pick the lessons and move on. Treat yourself the way you would treat another friend who was on a similar journey and needed your support. Seek help when you need it from people who are more experienced than you, and remember that it is okay to learn as you go. No one knows it all. Even the experts have something to learn from the up-and-comers. We are all learning. Adapt and learn from your shortcomings.

9. Remain teachable. Don't ever think that you know all there is to know about a skill. The world is ever-evolving, and new things are always coming up. Use every opportunity you find to learn from others. Don't stop learning.

10. Keep up with current events and changes in your industry. Keep an eye on trends. Join business associations. Subscribe to relevant newsletters. Stay current!

11. Share your knowledge, as this is one of the fastest ways to learn and improve. Volunteer your time in relevant associations. As you share what you know, you open yourself up to opportunities and you learn from others. You also make connections that will benefit your new season.

12. Network, network, network! Engage with others in your field. Getting the right things done the right way usually requires a combined effort. I couldn't complete my first contract on my own. I needed help from my neighbor to provide staffing for a role. Without this collaboration, I might have succumbed to the disappointment I felt and just abandoned the whole business. This shows that we achieve our goals faster when we collaborate with others. Be open to new strategic relationships. Build a culture of open communication, cooperation, and shared goals where you can work together to accomplish tasks with excellence.

13. Don't be in a hurry to grow. Sometimes we compare our journey with those of others who have been there way before we began. Remember that everyone's journey is different. And really, this is not a race to see who gets there first. Take your time to build and grow. Don't be in a hurry. A business that is built on a strong foundation will remain strong even in the face of trouble. But if we are in a hurry to expand, we risk losing all that we have worked for. Rushing to grow can lead to chaos and strain resources.

14. Practice effective time management. Time is your most scarce resource. You must learn to utilize it well by prioritizing tasks and delegating when needed. Set aside time for different crucial tasks, including strategic thinking. Utilize your time well and watch your business grow.

15. Find where your buyers are and go there, whether it is in business conferences or group hangouts. Several websites allow you to promote your business to ready buyers. Go on the internet, read reviews, see what

works, and place yourself in a position to be discovered by the right audience.

16. Celebrate progress and achievements. As you strive to get the right things done the right way, remember to celebrate your achievements. Acknowledge the progress you have made on your journey and let that fuel your desire to achieve excellence. Celebrating your achievements not only provides the motivation you need, but also reinforces the positive mindsets and habits that contribute to doing the right things the right way.

17. Have periodic reviews/reflections. Regularly assess your actions and decisions and consider whether they align with your values and contribute positively to the well-being of yourself and others. This helps you identify errors you may not have noticed. If done often, reflection gives you the chance to correct errors early.

Remember that you do not become a master in one day. It takes intentional actions, executed with excellence and mindfulness, to get to where you are going. Mastery is a continuous journey, a constant commitment to uphold your values, refine your skills, and contribute meaningfully to your work and the world around you. You may make mistakes on your way, but be quick to recognize them and put yourself back on track.

Here are some affirmations to inspire and support you as you start your journey and strive to do the right things right:

★ I am embarking on this new journey with an open heart and a clear mind.

★ Every step I take is a step towards progress and growth.

★ I trust in my ability to navigate this new path with wisdom and grace.

★ I am committed to learning and improving every day.

★ I embrace the unknown, knowing it brings new opportunities for success.

★ I have the strength to overcome challenges and stay on my path.

★ I am patient and persistent in pursuing my goals.

★ I am focused on doing things right, not just doing them quickly.

★ I trust my intuition and judgment as I make new decisions.

★ I am surrounded by positivity and support on this new journey.

★ I am capable of adapting to new situations with ease and confidence.

★ Every mistake is a learning opportunity that guides me to do better.

★ I am dedicated to living my truth and aligning my actions with my values.

★ I am constantly growing and evolving along this new path.

★ I approach each day with enthusiasm and a readiness to succeed.

★ I celebrate both small victories and big achievements on this journey.

★ I am resilient and can thrive through change and new beginnings.

★ I am grateful for this new opportunity to shape my future.

★ I have the power to create a positive and fulfilling journey.

★ I am a beacon of creativity, positivity, and determination on this new path.

CHAPTER 3

Love Yourself As You Love Your Neighbor

Lesson No. 3:

You are worthy of the same love, assistance, and compassion you give to others. You are enough and deserve to shine just as brightly as everyone else, so take care of yourself first. Self-love and self-care are not options. They're requirements.

My biggest lesson was learning how to stop people-pleasing. I was the poster child for constantly trying to please others. Too often, I sacrificed my own needs in the process. I was the classic fixer and always felt like I needed to "fix" or "rescue" someone because they "needed me." I thought if I just helped, their lives would be better. I didn't see it as being a people pleaser at the time. I saw it as loving people with the love of God—as doing God's work.

After abandoning myself time and time again, I was completely broken. Being a fixer didn't feel right anymore. I realized I'd been pouring into everyone else, but no one was pouring into me. My cup was empty, and I didn't know how to fill it up. I was so used to people taking energy from me that I failed to recognize I wasn't saving any for myself. My spirit was saying I was worthy, but I didn't feel worthy. The people I was pouring into didn't make me feel worthy of reciprocation. But it wasn't their responsibility. I was responsible for setting healthy boundaries and not giving more than I could afford to give. But I didn't know how to change the behavior. As a child, I didn't feel seen or heard, so I learned to fade into the background and take care of my own needs and those of others. I was a child who learned not to complain because it didn't matter. As an adult, I had to unlearn a lifetime of self-sabotaging behavior. I needed to heal from the childhood trauma that kept me stuck in a never-ending cycle of self-neglect, self-hate, and self-abandonment.

To heal my childhood trauma, I had to do some shadow work and rewrite the narrative of my life. I had to go back to the beginning and relive some painful memories I'd hidden deep inside of me, not daring to dredge them up because I didn't want to offend anybody by telling my truth. But I had to figure out why it was hard to set healthy boundaries and love myself. I needed to tell my story even if it was only to myself. I needed to heal my brokenness and gain self-worth, so I began writing . . .

My Story

My story isn't pretty. It's not all rainbows and sunshine where I have my whole life figured out. There's rain, gloom, thunderstorms, and lightning also. A voice screaming to be set free. A heart begging for love and acceptance. A mind constantly thinking of blue sky one minute and doubtful the next. Dreaming dreams grander than the eight wonders of the world but doubting that dreams like that could come true for a little black girl like me.

Picture a girl raised in the projects of Ponchatoula, Louisiana, by a poor single mother on welfare who had an eighth-grade education, six kids, and an abusive husband drunk off his own ego who was barely around. This little girl was physically, verbally, emotionally, and sexually abused by those around her. Could the little girl of that family become a success story? The unhealed version of me didn't believe I could. I'm supposed to be a product of my environment: a project chick, a hood rat, and a welfare recipient like my mother. I was supposed to be the girl who would drop out of high school because I got pregnant at the end of her eleventh-grade year. And I was supposed to be just a housewife because I decided to marry my son's father.

I'm not supposed to amount to anything because I'm the black sheep of the family, the one she wanted to give away because I was just another girl.

The one who was black as night. The black twin. I'm not supposed to dream bigger and think outside the box. That life wasn't for me. It was for other people. I'm supposed to put my head down and do as I'm told because my feelings and thoughts don't matter.

Those were the messages that were deep-rooted in my subconscious. They were planted by people around me. For most of my life, I actually believed them and lived my life accordingly. Why wouldn't I believe them? They were family. They were bosses. They were friends. They were adults. They were the people who claimed to love and care about me. I thought for certain they were right. Therefore, I needed to stop dreaming and thinking so big.

I allowed their negative thoughts, self-projection, jealousy, and envy to seep into my consciousness without question. I had unconsciously learned to shrink myself and to put others before me at a young age. That's where the self-hate, self-destruction, and brokenness began. I was conditioned to view myself as less than. To fade into the background because the life I wanted was for other people. Not me. They never truly saw me. Never understood me. Never allowed me to be free. They placed limits on my life before I knew my own worth. Therefore, I did the same. I engaged in self-sabotaging behavior because I didn't know that I was worthy of the life I wanted: a life where dreams do come true, a life where I didn't have to settle for whatever and whoever came my way. I didn't believe it was okay to serve and be served. I believed I was an indentured servant to everyone because I was the child who shouldn't have been born. The lies others told me, the lies I told myself, were countless.

I had to heal from that past trauma and learn how to love myself. Retelling my story gave me a new perspective on my soul's journey—the journey of discovering who I really am and not who everyone told me I was. I began to slowly dissect my past and unravel the truth that intertwined the lies.

The child who shouldn't have been

I'm the second to the youngest of my siblings. My parents had five girls and one boy. The boy is my twin, born fourteen minutes after me, which makes him technically the youngest child. My mother had her tubes tied three or four years prior to our birth. She didn't want any more kids but ended up pregnant with twins. Needless to say, she wasn't very happy about it. I was told she was ready to give me up for adoption to a pastor and his wife. My oldest sister begged my mom to keep me and promised to look after me. She was only ten at the time. When I heard this story, I was around five or six years old. I remember feeling sad, hurt, and unwanted. I couldn't understand at the time why she wanted to give me away and keep my twin brother. Why would anyone want to separate twins? How was it that my ten-year-old sister wanted me but my mother didn't? My dad wasn't around; therefore, I'd already formulated the thought of him not wanting me either. I was born to two parents who didn't want me; that was the story I told myself. It was heartbreaking. That was the first story that soon became deeply rooted inside of me. Every time my sisters told the story, it felt like a knife to my heart. It was a mockery. I felt ashamed, like the black sheep, the child who shouldn't have been born. That was the first time I felt unworthy. I wasn't worth having or keeping, or worthy of a parent's love. I wasn't supposed to be here anyway. Those words echoed in my mind over and over and over again.

As I got older, I couldn't decipher parental discipline from my own feelings of not being worthy. I would tell myself that every scolding and whipping I got was because she didn't want me. I went into people-pleasing mode, thinking maybe if I brought home good grades, was a good girl, and did what she said, she would want me and see my worth. But that's not what I felt. My mother wasn't affectionate. Her approach to parenting was very much hands-off: do as I say, not as I do; a child should be seen and not heard; I don't want to see you or hear you. Therefore, I often felt abandoned in my efforts and emotions.

Those feelings lingered into adulthood as I began seeking acceptance and self-worth from others. I started engaging in self-sabotaging behavior. I criticized myself about everything. I told myself I wasn't good enough for a healthy relationship, so I unconsciously settled for toxic ones because they mirrored my childhood. I tried to be perfect at everything, and if I couldn't make it perfect, I wouldn't do it at all. And when I did do something, impostor syndrome would kick in and I would shy away from compliments because I didn't want the attention out of fear that they were just being nice. It was hard to accept I was worthy of compliments and praise. I still have this struggle, but I've gotten better at it.

Black twin

I went to visit a friend one day. He introduced me to his mother, who was a lighter-skinned southern black woman. During our brief conversation, I told her I was a twin and that he was about her color and taller than me. Her response was unexpected and completely took me back to my childhood, in which my melanated skin wasn't celebrated in my household. As a child, I was told, "I'm gonna skin the black off of you," and called names like "tar baby" and . . . I'm still trying to figure out what a "black spazzard" is. Her words were just as cruel and diminishing: "Aw, he got the good genes," as if my black wasn't beautiful. It was colorism at its best.

Colorism is prevalent in the black community, especially in the South where racism has always existed. White is right and black is bad. The house nigger and the field nigger. Although we aren't slaves anymore, the mentality has been passed down from generation to generation. The false perception that the closer a black person is to white, the better they should be treated and the prettier or more handsome they are. The darker a black person is, the worse they are treated and the less likely they are to be seen as pretty or handsome.

I was born a twin. Out of all of my mother's kids, I am the darkest. My twin brother is lighter-skinned. When I was told the story of our birth, I was told my mother gave birth to a black baby and a white baby, not that she gave birth to two black babies. As we got older, his skin darkened, but he was still much lighter than me and considered a "redbone." My mom never uses the words *beautiful* and *black*, *brown*, or *dark* in the same sentence. It's typically "beautiful red," "pretty red," or "beautiful light-skinned."

Growing up, I didn't feel or know black was beautiful. I didn't think I was ugly, just not pretty like people who were lighter than me. I was told my hair was pretty, my clothes were pretty, and my shoes looked nice. But being called pretty or beautiful by my mother was not a thing. And when other people called me a "pretty black girl," my mother would divert the compliment instead of acknowledging or agreeing with it. "She's smart" or "don't tell her that" were her typical responses. Therefore, when I heard the words "He got the good genes," I was immediately disheartened. Not only did I feel like I had stepped back in time, but I felt like I couldn't escape my childhood trauma of feeling like I wasn't light enough or good enough for my mother. Those feelings seeped into my subconscious, and I found myself fading into the background when white or light-skinned people were around. That was how she treated me, so I believed it was what I was supposed to do. I was made to feel they were more important and valuable. I was taught to abandon myself for them. Even when I was in a relationship with someone who was white or almost white, my mother's empathy went to them, no matter how badly they treated me. She unconsciously projected her own fears, insecurities, and trauma onto me without realizing the effects they would have on my life. I had to learn to embrace my melanated skin and not allow anyone to make me feel like my black isn't beautiful..

The start of healing

I began telling myself I was beautiful instead of waiting to hear it from other people. I started to celebrate the skin I was born in and advocate for darker skin. I began accepting compliments with confidence and correcting people who would say, "You're beautiful for a black woman." I'm beautiful, and my skin is beautiful. I began embracing my African heritage, acknowledging the beauty of my black family and ancestors. I started embracing my kinky coils, thick lips, and all the things that make me who I am. I also made sure my son knew his black was beautiful. I wanted him to see himself the way I saw him and the way I wished my mom would have seen me.

I had to love myself first before others could love me. Self-care and self-love became my topmost priorities, and from loving myself, I began to project how others should treat me.

Many of us have unhealed trauma that affects our progress and the way we live our lives. Before you can make meaningful progress in business and life generally, you need to heal and unlearn any self-sabotaging behavior. These behaviors stop us from realizing our full potential and limit us in different areas of our lives.

Here are some ways you can unlearn a lifetime of self-sabotaging behavior and practice self-love:

1. **Practice self-awareness.** Take some time to reflect on your life and identify patterns of self-sabotage. Think about situations in the past where you have undermined your own well-being or success. It could be the way you respond to compliments because you don't believe them to be true. It could be self-doubt regarding your strengths and capabilities. There are several self-assessment resources online that you can use for this exercise. They help you discover traits that you may have been blinded to. Becoming self-aware of these traits is the first step to healing and becoming the powerful human God has called you to be.

2. **Understand the root cause.** A lot of the traumas we carry around come from our childhood. But then again, it could be from other events, which is why it is important to understand the root cause. What activities led you to where you are now? As a child, I didn't get the love of my family. I kept seeking validation from people. I wanted to be loved so badly that I tried to do everything right. So, even as an adult, I realized I was sacrificing myself to make others happy. I was investing in people who had no interest in me. To stop this cycle, I needed to understand the root cause and address it. I traced it to my childhood and was able to take steps to build my self-confidence and self-love actively. That made it easy to solve my self-love issues. Knowing the root cause of a thing makes it easier to solve. I know that this exercise may bring up painful memories or make you confront childhood demons, but it is necessary for your general well-being and growth.

3. **Decide to heal.** Tell yourself that you are ready to heal from the pain and hurt. Decide in your heart that you no longer want to sabotage your happiness. Commit to taking intentional steps toward your healing. Put in the work for your healing. Identify activities that will help you heal. Write them down and leave them in visible places so you are reminded of what you need to do. What can you do to feel better and be better? How can you love yourself more? How can you show up for yourself? How can you improve your mental health and not let the worries of the world pull you down? Your answers to these questions will make up your self-care and healing goals. Write down these goals and break them down into smaller, achievable steps to avoid being overwhelmed. Smaller goals are also easier to achieve and will build your sense of accomplishment.

4. **Challenge negative thoughts.** Negative thoughts come even to the best of men. The difference is between those who challenge their thoughts and those who accept them. Pay attention to your thoughts and replace negative thoughts with empowering and uplifting ones. If you think you can, you are correct. If you think you can't, you are also correct. The power lies in your hands.

5. **Develop healthy habits.** Start taking steps towards your healing. Create new habits that promote your overall well-being. These might include regular sleep, proper nutrition, exercise, affirmations, and mindfulness practices. Remember that you have to do something consistently for it to become a habit. Fill up your day with healthy activities until they become habits.

6. **Seek support.** We are designed as social beings for a reason. No man can do life alone. Find your own support system, whether they are family or friends, who you can share your struggles with. They can provide you with insights, different perspectives, and encouragement. They speak positively to your life when you are at your lowest. They show up for you and give you the needed motivation to continue. It could be one person or multiple people. What is most important is that you have them in your life.

7. **Learn stress management techniques.** Building a business and life itself can sometimes be stressful, so you need effective stress management techniques, like yoga, meditation, or deep breathing. Practicing these techniques can help you manage stress in healthier ways. Try different techniques to find the one you like best, and then stick with it.

8. **Celebrate your wins.** Sometimes, we are so consumed with our failures and struggles that we do not remember to celebrate our wins. You should acknowledge and celebrate every achievement, whether big or small. Taking the time to pat yourself on the back for your win gives your mind positive reinforcement and builds your confidence. Look at yourself in the mirror and mention how proud you are of you. Say it loud so your ears can hear it and your heart can believe it.

9. **Seek therapy or counseling.** Some of the battles we fight can only be won with the help of counseling or therapy. Therapies and counseling can

help you unload your struggles, acknowledge them, and heal from them. These are professionals with the skills to help you through every season of your life. Recently, some of these providers have introduced the option for you to interview your counselor before deciding to work with them. This allows you to choose the professional your spirit aligns with.

10. **Educate yourself.** There are many resources like this book that can help you heal and take charge of your life. Read self-help books, take personal development courses, and attend workshops. The more you educate yourself, the more you are able to challenge negative thoughts and liberate yourself.

11. **Create a positive environment.** What and who you surround yourself with will either make or mar you. Surrounding yourself with positive influences will keep you energized and motivated. Stay away from people who constantly pull you down or make you feel less worthy. Surround yourself with people who constantly remind you of your high value and worth—those who have the right message for you in the different seasons of your life.

12. **Forgive yourself.** While we do not plan to fail, we have to understand that failure is a part of life. Everyone makes mistakes. Dwelling on the mistake will not make it go away; rather, it demoralizes you and steals your joy. Forgive yourself for past mistakes and see them as learning opportunities for growth.

13. **Take breaks.** Life often gets so busy that we sometimes forget to stop and breathe. Take short breaks during the day to stretch, breathe, and revive yourself. Our minds need these breaks to continue to perform at top speed. Breaks are like mini vacations for your mind.

14. **Learn to accept compliments.** Don't brush them off. When you accept a compliment graciously, you are signaling to your mind that you know your worth. There is no modesty in rejecting compliments; you only end up harming your self-worth and mind. You deserve every genuine compliment you receive.

15. **Do things for you.** Life can get busy, but you must remain committed to practicing self-care. Take yourself out. Take a soak. Take walks in

the park. Talk beautifully to yourself. Do things that will improve your mental health. You will find more detailed and powerful self-care tips in chapter 7.

Remember that self-love requires continuous effort. It is not a one-time thing. Spend time with yourself and constantly invest in your personal development and growth. Be your biggest cheerleader. Celebrate the progress you make along the way, and be compassionate with yourself during the journey.

Here are some powerful affirmations to help build your self-love and self-worth. Recite them daily until they become a part of you:

★ I am deeply grateful for this life.

★ I am deserving.

★ This body accomplishes great things, and it is resilient.

★ I am mentally strong and capable of handling anything.

★ I make tough decisions and tackle difficult tasks when necessary.

★ I attract positivity like a magnet.

★ I am responsible, independent, and capable.

★ I have the power to choose happiness, joy, and positivity, and to love myself.

★ I promise to treat myself with kindness because I deserve it.

★ I am doing the best I can.

★ What needs to happen will happen.

★ I possess a unique gift that the world needs and deserves to witness.

★ I am unlike anyone else, and that is my greatest gift.

★ I give myself my own approval, the only approval I need.

★ What I bring to the table holds value.

★   My thoughts and ideas deserve to be acknowledged.

★   I am secure within myself.

★   I am confident in myself.

★   Good things await me, and positive experiences are on the horizon.

★   I am open to new and exciting experiences and opportunities.

CHAPTER 4

Riding the Wave of Entrepreneurship With Grace

LESSON NO. 4:

Keep going no matter how tough the road may get. Remember that tough times don't last; only those who persevere and are resilient will come out on top.

Many times, I hear people talk about entrepreneurship, and I wonder if they actually understand what the journey really entails. Many people romanticize entrepreneurship, seeing it as an escape from the 9-to-5 grind to build a glamorous life. People often see entrepreneurs as those who have successfully put their lives together and are on their way to success and freedom, but this is so far from the truth.

Although I enjoy what I do and how I connect people to their dream jobs, I can definitely say that I had fewer challenges working in my corporate job than I have faced running a business.

So in this chapter, I will share some struggles of entrepreneurship that people don't often talk about. I want to help you understand what the journey is like so that you can be gracious to yourself and other entrepreneurs you may meet on your way. I will also provide some helpful tips to help you navigate these challenges.

People see my success but don't know my struggles with entrepreneurship. There were times when I wanted to shut down the business because of stress or because I hadn't been producing revenue for months. Sometimes,

I didn't even have money to afford my personal or business expenses. I borrowed money without knowing how I would pay it back. Fighting through tears, depression, and feelings of defeat, I still got up every day and worked hard, yet I still couldn't produce enough revenue to sustain myself. At such times, nothing seemed to be working out. I thought maybe this was no longer what God wanted me to do. However, each time I prayed and would get down to my last few dollars, a door would open, and I'd push through.

There were people on what I like to call my support team who kept telling me to "keep going." But I was tired. I felt defeated and emotionally drained. I'd gotten to the point where all I could pray was, "Lord, read my heart because my mind can't formulate words right now. Amen." At one of my lowest points, one support team friend suggested I go into the community. She knew how much I enjoyed charity work. Although my spirits were down and my bank account was low, I signed up for another opportunity to volunteer. This time, it was to feed the homeless. It was cold and raining that day as we handed out warm food, drinks, and essentials to the homeless sleeping under the bridges and those less fortunate. At some point during the evening, I stopped to show gratitude to God because it was then I realized that even though I may be struggling with my finances and emotions, I'm still blessed. When we were done, I could go home to a warm home, bed, food, and other things we often take for granted. I was reminded of my "why"—why I started my business in the first place: to help people provide for their families. I got excited again. My heart became full by knowing what I was doing affected the lives of many in a positive way. It was the wind I needed to keep going.

As you continue your journey of entrepreneurship or embark on a new journey, here are a few tips to help you ride the waves of entrepreneurship with grace:

Riding the emotional rollercoaster

Entrepreneurship is just an emotional rollercoaster. You go from feeling so excited about landing your first client or officially starting your business to feeling low about harsh criticism or failed deals. The journey is filled with so many ups and downs that can lead to anxiety, stress, and burnout. While a salaried job guarantees you a fixed income, with entrepreneurship, you are not sure what to expect, even after you have done all you can to promote your business. Even the successful entrepreneurs you see today still face the emotional storms of this journey. The difference is that they have mastered or are mastering resilience. They are learning to bounce back from setbacks and push themselves to get to the level and goal they desire for their business.

If you are a business owner reading this or planning to start your own business, here are some helpful tips that will help you overcome this struggle:

- Practice mindfulness regularly to help you stay grounded. Mindfulness techniques like journaling or meditation can help in reflecting on and understanding your emotional responses. I meditate for ten minutes every day before I start work. If I begin to feel stressed during work, I sit still for a few minutes and concentrate on my breathing by taking at least five deep, slow breaths until I feel calm.

- Stay physically active. Studies have shown that regular exercise can help relieve stress. It's not just about staying fit but about creating a channel to release stress, anxiety and frustration. Mornings can be hectic for most people. Although I don't make it to the gym, I've made a habit of doing at least ten to twenty minutes of yoga before work. Usually, I do it before meditation. A healthy mind and body are important to entrepreneurship.

- Get adequate rest. I know that sometimes business needs may not leave much room for sleep, but you must intentionally get rest when your body needs it. Never underestimate the power of a good night's sleep. It helps to recharge and renew your mind, leaving you refreshed for the next day's tasks. Denying yourself sleep will only increase your emotional responses and impair your judgment. I've learned to give myself grace when I need to take a break, sleep in a little longer, or take a midday power nap. Your body gives you warnings before it shuts down, so listen to it.

- No man is an island, and that includes you. So commit to building a robust support system made up of mentors, fellow entrepreneurs, and supportive friends who understand your journey and can provide you with encouragement and the right advice. Seek mentors who have walked a similar path as you to get invaluable guidance and emotional support that will save you years of trial and error. They can be sounding boards for your fears and frustrations. Because they have walked the path you are currently on, they will save you from making the mistakes they made.

- Connect with other entrepreneurs who can relate to your experiences and share insights. The right peer group will provide you with advice, empathy, and a sense of community. You can find like-minded entrepreneurs through networking groups.

- Prioritize tasks and set realistic deadlines so you are not always rushing to meet deadlines. It is better to under-promise and over-deliver than to over-promise and then struggle to meet deadlines.

- Delegate and outsource when needed. You don't have to do everything by yourself. Ask for help and delegate tasks to reduce your workload. Consider teaming with other entrepreneurs in your field to accomplish tasks quicker. If you are a solopreneur, consider hiring an intern to help with small tasks so you can do what you do best.

- Take periodic breaks to help reset your mind and reduce your stress level. Go for a five- or ten-minute walk or step outside to get some fresh air.

- Have a positive mindset. This doesn't mean that you are wishing for the problems to go away or ignoring them. Rather, it's about maintaining a hopeful outlook that things will get better. Develop a mantra to repeat daily.

- If the emotional struggle becomes overwhelming, do not delay in seeking professional help. Consult with mental health professionals to help you manage anxiety, stress, and even depression. Therapy has helped me work through struggles related to business and personal matters.

Overcoming loneliness

Many entrepreneurs agree that the entrepreneurial journey can be lonely. Sometimes we are lonely because we have no one to share our worries and doubts with. We have people in our corner, but they may not understand the intricacies of our challenges. So we are left with either finding someone who can relate to our challenges or solve them ourselves. This kind of isolation is often a test of one's mental fortitude. At other times, we become lonely because we isolate ourselves (sometimes unintentionally) to do meaningful work, but this also means losing contact and connection with others.

Here are some tips to help you manage this struggle:

- Join entrepreneurial communities both online and locally to engage with other entrepreneurs. Platforms like Facebook, LinkedIn and industry-specific websites offer avenues for like-minded individuals to connect and support each other.

- Take part in networking events, workshops, and conferences, not only to expand your professional network but also to socialize with peers who are familiar with the entrepreneurial journey. Chapter 6 talks extensively about networking and how to do it right.

- Seek mentors who have a wealth of knowledge and are willing to share their insights with you. Remember that not all mentors are right for you. You want someone who is willing to hold your hand and walk the walk with you. You may even sign up for formal mentorship programs offered by many organizations and business groups. I see a lot of these groups on Facebook. Before signing up for these programs, check for their reviews and testimonials to help you know if they are right for you or not. Score.org is also a great resource for finding a mentor in your area and industry.

- If you have other people working with you, you can foster team connections by holding regular meetings to discuss work and connect on a personal level. Engaging in team-bonding activities can also help to encourage interaction and connection that go beyond work-related tasks.

- I know that life can get too busy when building a business, but you must create time to socialize with others. What will help is scheduling time to socialize, just as you schedule work tasks. Whether it is attending a hobby class or going on a weekly dinner with friends, make social time a non-negotiable part of your calendar.

- You could use a co-working space rather than working from home all the time. This allows you to work and also interact with others. We all love working from home, but it can be lonely being indoors all the time. This arrangement helps you achieve both benefits.

- Don't lose touch with family and friends because you are building a business. You will one day need them to hold you up. So, get them involved in what is happening. At first, you may need to do a lot of explaining to help them understand the work you do, but it is worth it at the end of the day. Share business ideas with them and seek their opinion. Let them know about your challenges and experiences. Sharing your journey and getting loved ones involved helps lessen the feeling of isolation.

- Seek opportunities to collaborate with other entrepreneurs or businesses on projects or events. Collaborating with others will not only reduce loneliness but also open doors to new relationships.

- Create your own support group or join existing online groups for entrepreneurs facing similar challenges. If you can't find the right group, it means there is a gap you can fill by creating a group that addresses your needs. Others like you are searching for such groups and will join if you create one. You can choose to keep the group as an online forum or have monthly in-person meetings.

- Protect your mental health. Avoid things and situations that will compromise your mental health. Seek help from mental health professionals to help you combat loneliness.

- Get involved in your local community by volunteering or participating in community projects as a way of giving back and enjoying social interactions.

- Join local business associations or chambers of commerce for both business development opportunities and social interactions.

- Take time regularly to check in with yourself. How are you feeling? Do you feel like you are still in touch with others, or are you out of touch? What can you do to feel more connected? The answers to these questions will help you address any issues that need to be addressed.

Becoming a better decision-maker

As an employee, all I did was do my job right and support my team members; the people at the top made the business decisions. Now, as a business owner, I have to make tough decisions amidst the constant fear that I may make the wrong one. Every decision in entrepreneurship feels magnified. From choosing the right team members to making financial investments, each choice we face is a weight that can be overwhelming. The first step in managing this struggle is understanding that decisions must be made. The next step then becomes putting in place structures to ensure you are making the right decisions as much as possible. Here are some tips to help you make better business decisions.

- Have a structured approach to making decisions; this will be your decision-making framework. List specific criteria any decision must meet, including factors like resources, costs, time, and alignment with your business goals. When setting up your decision-making framework, use business models like cost–benefit analysis, SWOT analysis (Strengths, Weaknesses, Opportunities, Threats), or the Eisenhower matrix, also known as the time management matrix. The models guide you in setting a realistic framework that considers every important factor in your business.

- Conduct thorough research before making a decision, including financial forecasts, market research, feedback from clients or team members, and expert opinions. Consult with your mentors or experts in the field for their experience-based insights. This way, you are sure you are making informed decisions.

- Use data analytics tools to gain insights from existing data, and make your decisions based on these insights. Everything you are doing now has been done in the past, and there is almost always data you can use in identifying trends, forecasting outcomes, and making data-backed decisions.

- You may not always have time to check data. In such cases, trust your gut feeling. Pay attention to your instincts, especially if you've gained some years of experience in the business.

- Have a clear deadline for making a decision to prevent procrastination and indecision. Sometimes, the longer time you take to make a decision, the harder it becomes to actually make the decision.

- Have backup plans in case the decision doesn't work out as expected. Knowing you have a backup plan will reduce the pressure you may feel when making that decision.

- Avoid overanalyzing situations. Know that you cannot always have all the information you want to make a decision. Rather than overanalyzing, focus on the business's overall goals and objectives and let them guide you in making decisions that align with your long-term vision.

- Make your decisions when you are calm and composed. Take brief walks, take a deep breath, or engage in meditation to help you relax and get in the best frame of mind for making decisions. Maintaining a healthy lifestyle, like sleeping well, exercising regularly, and eating right, also enhances your decision-making skills.

- If you have other people working with you, involve them in making business-related decisions. This opens you up to new perspectives you may not have considered, and it also makes the team feel valued. You may also delegate the process to a trusted team member with more expertise in that area.

- Analyze the outcome of every decision, reflecting on what worked and didn't work and why. Use the reflections to refine your decision-making process for the future. Seek feedback from team members and external stakeholders on the impact of the decision on them and their business.

Overcoming the fear of failure

Perhaps one of the fears every one of us has in common is the fear of failure. We are all afraid to fail because of what people will say or do. So, we limit the risks we take and, in the process, limit the business's growth potential. Here are some tips that have helped me overcome this fear.

- The first step is to know what is behind the emotion. Our fear often stems from a combination of societal pressures, self-doubt, and past experiences, and these are all valid fears that are not specific to business owners alone. Knowing the root cause helps make it easy for you to address it.

- Change the way you see failure. That something didn't work out doesn't mean you are a failure. It is all about your perception. If you see failure as an opportunity to learn and grow, fear will lose its control over you. Failure is not a death sentence but rather an opportunity to find other ways to do the same thing. Read about the journeys of successful entrepreneurs who have failed in the past to inspire and remind yourself that failure is often part of this entrepreneurial journey.

- Set achievable and realistic goals. We sometimes create very lofty goals to compete with similar businesses that have been operating since long before we entered the market. When we don't meet these lofty goals, we begin to think we have failed. You haven't failed, you only had unrealistic goals. Break your big goals into smaller, manageable objectives, and as you meet each objective, you build your confidence and overcome your fear.

- Celebrate every growth you achieve on your journey, whether big or small. This will help eliminate fear and boost your confidence and trust in yourself.

- Be ready to learn from your journey. Embrace challenges and see them as opportunities to expand your knowledge or skills. If you didn't get something right the first time, find other ways to do it better.

- Let your focus be on the effort you put in rather than the outcome. Knowing that you put in all necessary effort reduces the pressure of failing. You can give something your best and it may still not work out. That is because of the constant change in the business world. Don't beat yourself up over it.

- Speak to yourself with love and grace. Recite the affirmations in each chapter of this book to build your confidence and self-grace.

- Share your fears with your mentors, peers, or mental health professionals to provide you with relief and new perspectives.

- Accept that entrepreneurship is filled with uncertainty, and focus on only what you can control. Channel your resources and energy on the aspects of your business that are within your influence rather than worrying about factors outside your control.

- While striving for the best outcome, also prepare for different outcomes. This will help reduce the anxiety associated with uncertainty.

- Engage in activities that build resilience, like physical exercise or skills development. Building your resilience will help you bounce back from failures and setbacks.

- Analyze what went wrong, and identify better ways to approach similar situations in the future. Then use these insights to improve your strategies.

- Encourage creativity within the group. The fear of failure stifles creativity, but if you encourage creativity and allow team members to experiment with different strategies, you will end up teaching them that failure is a part of the process.

- Prioritize your self-care so that you are always in the right frame of mind when and if failure happens. Sleep well, eat well, and exercise frequently for your general well-being.

- Seek constructive feedback from colleagues, customers, and others who know you. Seeking and receiving feedback provides you with a different perspective and highlights areas for improvement you may not have considered.

- Surround yourself with others who understand the challenges of running a business. Stay in touch with your mentors and peers to receive emotional support and practical advice at all times.

Maintaining a good work-life balance

Work on balancing your personal and professional lives. Most salaried workers can psychologically leave work at closing, but this is often hard for a business owner. Business owners struggle with balancing their work lives and their personal lives because they are constantly thinking of how to grow their businesses. We channel all our time and energy into growing the business, often leaving us too tired to socialize or even take care of ourselves. This is especially true in the first few years of the business, where you are trying to grow awareness of your brand and break even. The imbalance sometimes strains our friendships and relationships with people who matter. It often leads to lost relationships and even personal dissatisfaction. I, too, struggled with balancing my business and personal lives. But does work–life balance mean having an equal split between your work and personal lives? No, this term means finding harmony between both lives to avoid burnout. When you are pulled from different directions, and you have no strategy on the ground to navigate the demands of both your work life and your personal life, you will end up burned out, frustrated, and unable to give the best of yourself to both worlds. So here are some of the tips I found helpful.

- Define your work hours and try as much as possible to stick to these hours. There will be times when you will need to go beyond the set hours, but creating a routine like this lets others know when you are available for work-related matters.

- It also helps if you have a designated area in your home for work. This helps in mentally separating work from your personal life. There is this awareness when you walk into the assigned space at the beginning of work or leave the space at the end of the day. It's similar to how you feel in a traditional job when you leave the building to head home.

- Learn how to prioritize tasks, focusing mainly on tasks only you can handle and delegating the other tasks to reduce work pressure. You will find several tools, like the Eisenhower Matrix, that will help you categorize tasks based on their importance and urgency. Using this method will ensure you do not spend so much time and energy doing unimportant or non-urgent tasks. If a task can be outsourced or delegated, find a trusted and skilled person to handle it. Always remind yourself that you don't have to do everything yourself.

- Look for apps and tools that enhance productivity, such as automation tools, project management software, and time-tracking applications. One of the beautiful automations I enjoy using is a tool for scheduling meetings. For example, with Calendly, clients can book an appointment with you and the app will automatically share your meeting link with them. At the end of the meeting, the app can also send a follow-up or thank-you message to the attendees. This app can be used for both one-on-one meetings and group meetings. This one app saves me a lot of manual effort.

- Embrace technology, but also have limits in place to ensure you don't go overboard. Technology can be a blessing but also a curse if not used correctly. Have a defined time for checking emails and messages to avoid the temptation of being constantly available. You will be tempted to check your emails at all times, but if you create a time block and stick to it, you will find it easier to follow as time goes on.

- No matter how busy work may be for you, always have a non-negotiable personal time. Intentionally block time in your calendar for non-work activities like spending time with friends and family or pursuing a hobby.

- Take regular short breaks throughout the day to rest and recharge. Again, you must be intentional about this to avoid burnout.

- Let clients, employees, and partners know your availability and response time to manage their expectations. Some people will still contact you outside your communicated available hours. If you keep making yourself available at these times, they will not learn to respect your availability.

- Be careful not to over-commit. Know your limit and what you can achieve in a given time frame. Don't take more jobs than you can handle to avoid burnout, frustration and leaving a negative impression.

- Your health should always be your number one priority; after all, only a living and healthy person can work and grow their business. Ignoring your health can cause severe consequences. See your health as your most valuable asset, and treat it as such by exercising regularly, sleeping well, eating the right food, and practicing mindfulness and relaxation. Practices like yoga, meditation, or even just spending time in nature can help reduce stress levels significantly.

- Learn to say no. Many people struggle with this, including me. As an entrepreneur, you will encounter many opportunities, but not all of them are worth pursuing. Be intentional about the projects and commitments you take on. Check whether the requirements align with your business vision or are a good fit for you, and say no to less important projects or projects that require more than you can handle so that you can have the time and strength to focus on things that truly matter.

- Know that your time is a precious gift from God, and you must be judicious about how you spend it. Do not spend your time on things that add no value to you or your business. You will receive many messages from people seeking to speak with you about various things. Ask yourself if there is any value-add to both you and the other person. Then there are those people who will constantly come to you for free service. Know when to say no and maximize your time for more rewarding activities.

- Build a supportive network to ease the burden that comes with owning a business. Maintain your relationship with friends and family, as they can provide you with a sense of grounding as well as emotional support. Build a network of other entrepreneurs, professional advisors, and mentors who can share the workload, offer advice, or even lend a sympathetic ear.

- Have your business goals and also your personal development goals. Identify areas for personal growth, and set goals to achieve them. The goal could be improving your physical fitness, learning a new skill, or trying a new hobby. It doesn't matter how big or small the goal may be.

What is most important is that you are growing as an individual along with your business.

- Take time off work to recharge and reboot. Schedule your vacations and stick to them. While on vacation, be sure to disconnect from work completely to enjoy the full benefits of the time off. If you cannot afford a long vacation, consider shorter breaks like staycations or weekend getaways. No matter how long, take time away from work, and you will return feeling refreshed and recharged. Work will be there when you get back.

- One benefit of owning a business is that you control your hours. You can choose working hours that align with your commitments and personal productivity patterns. Schedule your working hours to suit your family time and other commitments you may have. This way, you can maintain your relationships while still working full hours.

- Take some time each day to meditate on the things you are grateful for. Focusing on the things that are working well in your life will improve your mood and shift your perspectives on life. Be thankful for the lessons learned.

- If you still cannot balance your work and personal lives, reach out for professional help. A counselor or therapist can help you create strategies that will work for you.

Overcoming self-doubt and impostor syndrome

Now, this is my favorite—overcoming self-doubt and impostor syndrome. Even as I grow and progress in business, I still battle with overcoming the feeling that I am not deserving of my success. Am I really as good as I think I am? Do I really have what it takes to build this business to my dream heights? These are some questions entrepreneurs often ask themselves, leading to self-doubt and hindering decision-making. Many entrepreneurs, regardless of their success, often have to deal with feelings of inadequacy and fear of being exposed as frauds even though they are authentic and know their worth. Here are tips to manage this struggle:

- You need to understand that you are not alone in this struggle. A lot of people, whether business owners or C-level professionals, have this same problem. Understanding that impostor syndrome is common and acknowledging its presence is your first step in addressing it.

- Take time to reflect on all you have achieved. One way you can do this is to record your successes, both big and small. These could include awards, recognitions, certifications, continuing education, networking events attended, new relationships, milestones reached, projects completed, and new skills. Then, whenever impostor syndrome creeps in, go through your log to remind you of your capabilities.

- Celebrate all your milestones, big and small. Starting and growing a business is no mean feat, so every time you hit a first in your business, celebrate it—whether it is getting your own logo, signing up your first client, or even having your website up. Celebrate every win you make in this journey. This helps reinforce a sense of accomplishment and competence.

- Acknowledge that you cannot know everything about your business. You have to commit to constantly learning and improving yourself. Read every resource there is in your field, ask questions if you don't understand, seek those who know more than you, and ask them to mentor you.

- Entrepreneurship comes with a lot of risk and uncertainty, and there is nothing you can do about this. Accept this uncertainty and know that it has nothing to do with your capabilities.

- Actively challenge negative thoughts as they come to mind. Ask yourself if these thoughts are based on unfounded fears or facts. You will find that most of the negative thoughts are based on fear of what people will say or do or think. Fill yourself with positive affirmations. You will find affirmations at the end of each chapter in this book. Declare them to yourself until you believe them. Never stop declaring these affirmations to build your confidence and self-worth.

- When you think you are not deserving of something, seek feedback from trusted mentors, peers, or colleagues who know you and can attest to your skills. They will provide you with a more objective view of your achievements and abilities. A mentor who has walked a path similar to yours can also provide comfort and reassurance about your entrepreneurial journey.

- Talk with others about your feelings of self-doubt. Sharing your fears and feelings with the right people can be incredibly liberating and validating. It also allows others to share their struggles with you so you know you are not alone on the journey.

- Seek professional counseling if the feeling gets overwhelming. A counselor or therapist will work with you to identify the reasons behind such feelings and help you overcome them.

- Be realistic about your goals. I know we like to dream big, and there is nothing wrong with dreaming big, but to achieve your big dreams, you need to break your goals into small, achievable actions. If you fail at one goal, try again. Keep trying until you get it. Mistakes are a natural part of the process, and so is failure. It has nothing to do with your worth or ability. Even the most successful entrepreneurs have had their share of failures.

- Focus on your strengths rather than your weaknesses to boost your self-confidence. Regularly assess your strengths and find ways to use them in your business. Find creative ways to develop your strengths and gain new skills. With each skill you add, you improve your self-confidence and business performance.

- Read about other entrepreneurs who experienced and overcame self-doubt and impostor syndrome. Examples include Sheryl Sandberg, David Bowie, Serena Williams, Howard Schultz, and so many others. Their stories will provide you with comfort and strategies to deal with your own feelings.

- Seek support groups for entrepreneurs where everyone openly shares their struggles and supports each other.

- Show love to yourself just as you would to others. Talk to yourself as if talking to a friend in a similar situation. Sometimes we are kinder to others than we are to ourselves. You are your number one friend, so be kind and practice self-compassion.

- Think about all the challenges you've faced and how you bounced back each time. Here is another situation where you want to keep records. Keep a journal where you reflect on past challenges and how you overcame them. This will remind you of your resilience and resourcefulness.

- See every challenge as a learning opportunity rather than an opportunity to berate yourself. Accept that failure is part of the journey of growth. You will fail more than you would like, but it will only make you a better person and a better entrepreneur.

- Don't be in a hurry to achieve perfection. Take it one day at a time, and celebrate your progress as you go.

Navigating changes

The only constant in business is change. Trends are always changing, and so are consumer behaviors and technology, and keeping up with these changes can be very exhausting. Business owners have to follow the trends constantly if they want to remain relevant. Here are some tips to help you effectively adapt to the ever-changing business landscape:

- Accept that change is part of the process. Adaptability starts with your mindset. Having a mindset that accepts change as an integral part of business is necessary for your survival. See change as your opportunity to learn and grow. Be open to trying new ideas and approaches. This will help you adapt quickly and turn challenges into valuable learning experiences.

- Take time to research emerging trends in your industry. Do this no more than once or twice a week to avoid being overwhelmed by information overload. This research can be done through attending conferences, reading industry publications, or taking part in online forums. Also, you need to network with other professionals in your field to exchange knowledge and information as well as to learn about how they are adapting to the changes in the industry. Staying abreast of industry trends will make you better prepared for any change in the industry.

- Encourage your team to come up with new ideas and solutions for your business. Find different ways to remain innovative so that you are not left out of industry growth. Recognize and reward team members who have innovative ideas even if you don't end up using their ideas. This will encourage them and others to continue to find ways to improve your business processes.

- Implement agile project management techniques in your business operations. These techniques, which emphasize collaboration, flexibility, and rapid response to change, allow businesses to respond quickly and efficiently to change.

- Hold regular meetings with your team to review team progress and identify areas for improvement. This will help to ensure you are prepared for change with effective strategies that will keep your business moving forward.

- Invest in training and development for yourself and others on your team, whether free or paid training. Several online learning platforms offer free or low-cost training that you can utilize to develop yourself. Examples include Udemy, Skillshare, LinkedIn Learning, Coursera, Thinkific, and edX.

- New technologies are released every day. Adopt the ones relevant to your industry. Ensure you are on the right digital platforms and adopt new software or tools used by others in your industry. The goal is to stay tech-savvy. Consider how you can use these tools to improve and streamline your operations. Thankfully, most of these tools help reduce inefficiency and improve productivity.

- Change often comes with its own risk, so before you make a change, conduct risk assessments to ensure you are going in the right direction or implementing the right decision for your business. Have contingency plans in place for different scenarios so that even if the change fails, your business operations will not be significantly affected.

- Review your business plan regularly to ensure it is updated and adaptable to changes in your business environment and your industry.

- Have your long-term business goals, but have short-term goals as well so you have the flexibility to adapt and pivot when needed.

- Seek regular feedback from your customers, as that will let you know where the trend is heading. Customer feedback is a great source of information for adapting to change. It highlights areas for improvement and potential market shifts.

- If you haven't already, invest in building a social media presence for your business. Use social media platforms to engage with both existing and potential clients and to gain insight into their preferences and behaviors.

- As your team enlarges, bring in people with diverse skills and backgrounds to provide a range of solutions and perspectives. Provide your team with the right training and resources that will help develop their adaptability skills.

- Change can be stressful, so as you navigate through the ever-changing business terrain, prioritize your emotional and mental well-being and that of your team members. Build a work environment where team members are comfortable discussing and sharing their struggles and challenges related to change. Encourage practices like meditation, mindfulness, and regular physical activity to manage stress.

- Always keep your customers' needs top of mind when implementing changes. Constantly assess and understand the changing needs of your customers and ensure your services can meet these needs. Also, ensure your changes or innovations align with improving customers' experience with your brand.

Financial management

Managing financial uncertainty is another struggle every businessperson faces. Not being able to guarantee a minimum amount of income per month is a significant stressor, especially for new businesses. Unlike the regular paycheck traditional employees receive, an entrepreneur's income is often unpredictable. Today you may earn high, and tomorrow you earn nothing. Entrepreneurs have less control over their income than traditional employees. This uncertainty often causes financial stress and doubts, especially if the delay in earning income stretches beyond what one's savings can cover. Here are some tips on how you can effectively manage financial instability and associated risks:

- Have a detailed and well-thought-out financial plan, and budget for all potential expenses and revenues. Review your budget often to ensure it matches actual financial performance.

- Monitor your cash flow and understand your cash flow patterns. Your cash flow pattern shows you how cash comes in and leaves your business. This understanding will guide your decisions on investments, expenses, and growth strategies.

- Have an emergency fund you can fall back on should your business not generate enough income to cover your operating expenses. The emergency fund should be able to cover at least six months' worth of business expenses. Financial advisors recommend you have this emergency fund before resigning from your paid employment. While this is the best advice, what happens if you lose your job before you have enough savings? Then, you would need to build your emergency fund gradually by setting aside some amount consistently, no matter how little, as you start and grow your business. You can invest part of your business profit in building your emergency fund. This may mean not paying yourself a salary for some months until you have achieved this goal.

- Find other ways to generate income for your business. This could be offering new products or services, adopting a different sales strategy, or expanding into new markets. Creating multiple sources of income for your business means you are able to serve your customers in different ways or serve different customers in the same way. This way, you are doing more and earning more.

- Consider passive sources of income that don't require your full attention, like investing in real estate, hedge funds, or other financial market funds that an investment advisor can manage.

- Keep a record of your expenses and review it periodically to identify areas where costs can be optimized or reduced. Search for cost-effective alternatives for the services and products you use. This may mean changing suppliers, changing software type, or outsourcing certain tasks. If you are using a team software plan, for example, and only one team member is using that plan, consider switching to an individual plan and saving some money. With globalization, you may reduce your costs by outsourcing certain tasks to someone in a different country or region. Find creative ways to operate at the lowest cost possible without compromising on quality.

- Explore various funding options available for entrepreneurs, such as loans, crowdfunding, investors, or grants. Choose the option that is best for your business and review the terms thoroughly before applying. Build your credit rating, and establish and maintain good relationships with banks and other financial institutions so you can have access to additional capital when needed.

- Periodically assess your business risks and build strategies to manage them. These risks could be market risks, financial risks, compliance risks, or operational risks. Not managing them well and on time could cause more harm and financial expense to your business. Once you identify all possible risks, develop the right strategies to mitigate them. Some effective strategies include purchasing insurance, implementing strict compliance protocols, or diversifying suppliers.

- Ensure you have the right insurance package for your business. There are several kinds of insurance available to business owners and their businesses. Speak with your financial advisor about the best kinds for you, like property insurance, liability insurance, or professional indemnity insurance. But don't just stop at getting the insurance. Ensure you regularly review your insurance needs and update your coverage as your business grows. This way, you are sure of getting the best coverage for your business.

- Stay informed about market trends to help you expect and prepare for possible financial changes. Conduct market research to understand industry trends, competitive dynamics, and economic conditions that will affect your business, and be prepared to adapt your business strategies to respond to market changes in a way that will keep your business competitive and financially viable.

- Take time to learn about financial management, financial analysis, and accounting principles. While you may have an accountant or financial advisor managing your finances, understanding these principles will help you make better financial decisions. Ask your financial professionals to explain terms and principles to ensure you are financially literate.

- Track your finances, analyze financial data, and manage your invoices using financial management software. This will not only save you time but also reduce errors from manual computation. There are free online tools you can use, such as Wave and PayPal.

- Automate routine financial processes like invoicing, payroll, and billing to save time and reduce errors.

- Be clear about your payment terms. Is it full payment before service or payment after service? If it is payment after service, what is the payment duration? Ensure that these credit terms are clearly spelled out and enforced consistently to ensure timely payment. Assess the creditworthiness of both new and existing customers to reduce the risk of payment defaults.

- Build a business model that can withstand and adapt to any financial changes. Make sure your business processes are flexible and scalable, allowing for adjustments to be made in times of financial difficulty.

- Monitor key financial metrics like cash flow ratios, profit margins, and return on investment to ensure you are making the right financial decisions for your business. These metrics will signal whether you are making a profit or incurring a loss and will help you identify the need to either increase your pricing or scale back your offer.

Managing the unknown and unknown unknowns

Lastly, entrepreneurship doesn't come with any step-by-step manual, so each entrepreneur is left with navigating the tides and discovering what works for their business after many trials and errors, mistakes, and losses. This uncertainty can sometimes discourage people from continuing, especially in the first few years of the business life cycle. Here are some tips to help you embrace and manage the unknown in your entrepreneurial journey:

- Accept that you can't control everything. Have a mindset that welcomes new challenges and sees every challenge as an opportunity to gain new knowledge and skills. Each time I face a challenge, I take my lessons from the challenge and come out better than before.

- Be flexible in your planning, ready to adapt and adjust as needed to whatever situations you may experience.

- Do not rely on a single product or service, if possible. Create various ways of offering the same service to your customers. Expand your offer with related services.

- Identify potential risks and put plans in place to mitigate and manage these risks. When conducting your risk assessments, remember to consider both internal and external factors. Although the external factors are outside your control, knowing them will help prepare you to manage them effectively. Have a contingency plan for managing each identified risk. This plan will detail what your response would be should each risk materialize. This way, you are able to respond swiftly when faced with uncertainties.

- Don't restrict yourself or your team to one way of doing things. Try different ways, and freely experiment with new ideas until you find better ways of doing things. This could involve regular brainstorming sessions or innovation workshops.

- Stay updated on industry trends to gain insight and be better prepared for changes. When you are prepared for what is to come, you can change a negative situation into a positive one.

- Maintain a healthy cash flow to manage unexpected expenses. Maintain good relationships with financial institutions and potential investors so you can get financial help when needed.

- There are so many technological advancements in the world you can use to your advantage. Invest in these technologies to reduce costs, improve efficiency and stay competitive. Be among the first adopters of new technologies or tools. Be open to trying and adopting new technologies that will improve your business operations or expose you to new markets.

- Build a network of contacts across various professions and industries for varied perspectives and solutions. This way, you can seek feedback from others outside your industry to gain insight into potential clients' behaviors and needs.

- Reach out to successful entrepreneurs who have walked the path that you are on and ask them to mentor you. Don't stop seeking a mentor until you get one who is dedicated to your success. Their insights in navigating challenging times will make it easier for you to manage and overcome difficult situations in your business.

- Attend seminars and webinars, take courses, and read extensively in areas connected to your business and personal growth. Be committed to your personal development and growth. This will equip you with the right skills and knowledge to adapt to change. Seek every opportunity to learn from others, through industry conferences, workshops, or webinars where experts share their experience and knowledge with others.

- Maintain an open line of communication with your clients and every other stakeholder. By doing this, you build transparency and trust within your network. This also gives your stakeholders the opportunity to provide you with the best support and collaboration. If you have people on your team, keep them in the loop of any potential changes that may occur to encourage a collaborative approach to finding solutions.

- Building your emotional intelligence can help you manage your reactions to changes and maintain clear thinking. It starts with knowing how you respond to uncertainty and then increasing your emotional intelligence to where you are better able to respond to uncertainties. Maintain a clear head so you can make the best decisions for your business at all times.

- Never underestimate the effects your well-being has on your ability to handle critical situations. Rest well, eat well and exercise frequently. You want to be mentally, physically and emotionally fit so you can be prepared to act when needed. Take time off work to recharge and commit to achieving a good work–life balance.

- Consider all the scenarios that could play out for your business and the wider market, ranging from best case to worst case. Then plan for each scenario, outlining how best you would respond to it.

Entrepreneurship is a test of not only your knowledge and skills but also your mental and emotional strength. Business owners must cultivate a resilient, strong, and adaptive mindset to remain standing through the struggles of the entrepreneurial journey. And above all, pray about your journey and plans and ask God to help you make the right decisions and meet the right people who he would use to take you to your next level in business.

Here are some powerful affirmations to declare over your business. Declare them every day, every time and watch your mindset change for good as well as enjoy good progress:

★ My business is thriving.

★ I have unwavering belief in myself and trust in my abilities to succeed in all of my endeavors.

★ Success comes naturally to me, and I effortlessly attract wealth and happiness.

★ The work I do makes a significant difference.

★ I am intelligent and accomplished.

★ I can achieve any business goals I set for myself.

★ I consistently create wonderful opportunities in my industry.

★ My income is constantly and rapidly increasing. As I continue to achieve more success, I can help more people.

★ My passion for my business shines through in everything I do.

★ I effortlessly attract sales and my ideal clients.

★ My business allows me to live a life that I absolutely love.

★ I am full of energy and enthusiasm for my business.

★ The freedom my business provides me is something I cherish.

★ My business dreams continuously manifest into reality.

- ★ I am a perfect match for the business I have always desired.

- ★ I am grateful for the opportunities that come my way, as well as for every person who contributes to the success of my business.

CHAPTER 5

Spotlighting Your Business

LESSON NO. 5:

Engage actively with your market. This means understanding your audience, leveraging the right promotional tools, crafting compelling messages, and consistently evaluating the effectiveness of your strategies.

One need every entrepreneur has in common is the need to grow their business, and one sure way of achieving this is by promoting your business. You may have the best service, but if nobody knows about you and your services, no one will patronize you. Whether you are a small business or a large enterprise, the power of effective promotion cannot be overstated.

In today's competitive market, one needs to use both traditional and innovative strategies in their promotion plan to get to the intended audience. There are probably several other businesses doing the same thing as you. Using multiple promotional methods is one way you can differentiate yourself in a saturated market. There are several staffing and recruiting firms in Texas, especially in the Greater Houston Area. One difference between each one of us is how far and wide we can promote our business.

In addition to promoting your business, look for ways to increase your visibility as an entrepreneur. People want to do business with people they know and trust. As a new entrepreneur in a city I didn't grow up in, I didn't have the luxury of people knowing who I am. So I began attending networking events hosted by local and national government agencies and large corporations. The Small Business Administration (SBA), the Minority Business Development Agency (MBDA), SCORE, and minority certifying agencies offer various business workshops and events. Other ways I have increased my visibility include setting up booths at job fairs and getting profiled in magazines.

Now I will provide you with some tools that I have used and will continue to use to promote my business.

1. **Understand your audience.** This is the very first activity you must conduct before you start any marketing activities. If you know who your audience is, what their needs are, and how you can meet them, you will be able to create promotional campaigns that will appeal to them and encourage them to take your desired action. To understand your audience, conduct market research to identify your target demographics and learn about their preferences, needs, and pain points. Then build marketing strategies that will suit your audience. For example, what will move older adults will likely not appeal to younger adults because of differences in preferences and needs. So you must know who your audience is and what they seek to get from your product.

2. **Develop a strong brand.** Most times, when people hear the word *brand*, they associate it with just the business name and logo, but a brand is more than these two elements. It's about the customer's experience with your business through all your touch points. Your brand is what customers think and know of you. It is what comes to the minds of the audience when your business name is mentioned.

    •   It starts with your brand identity. Your brand identity is the visible element of your business, including your logo, colors, your business name, typography, and design. These elements help clients identify your business. You must ensure the elements of your brand identity work together to support your business values and goals.

    •   The next is your brand image. This is what people think about your business—your customers' perception of who you are and what you are about. These perceptions come from their experiences with the brand, your marketing efforts, and word of mouth. You want to strive for a positive image as much as you can manage that.

- The next element of your brand is your brand personality. Just like humans, your brand can have a personality. You see a brand's personality in the colors in their designs and the tone of voice in their marketing materials. It could be playful, youthful, professional, adventurous, and so on. The right brand personality depends on the demographics of your audience. A brand hoping to attract young people will have a youthful, playful personality, while a brand that is designed for experienced adults and C-level executives will often go for a professional personality. Identifying your audience will guide you in creating the right personality for your business.

- The fourth element is your brand culture and values. These are your core values, what you stand for. Examples include customer service, commitment to high quality, sustainability, innovation, safety, community involvement, and so on. These are values that often resonate with your target audience, and they must see them in your daily operations.

- The fifth element is brand experience—the sum of every interaction or touch points the audience has with your brand. Is your website easy to navigate and use? Does your business prioritize customer service? Do your clients feel heard? Are complaints resolved on time? Are your social media pages organized and friendly? Your audience will rate their experience with your brand based on all the touch points they interact with. A negative experience on one channel may cause customer dissatisfaction and affect your brand, but a positive brand experience will always build loyalty and generate more word-of-mouth marketing for you.

- The sixth element is brand differentiation. Every business has to find one thing that differentiates it from its competitors. Why should your customers patronize you and not your competitor? What value do you offer that they cannot find elsewhere? This is your Unique Selling Proposition. It's what makes your brand stand out and can include your product quality, features, pricing, customer service, etc.

- Next is brand communication. This is how you interact and communicate with your customers. What channels can your audience find you on? It could be through social media, content marketing, advertising, public relations, and so on.

All these elements combine to form your brand. Build a powerful brand that shows your core values, mission, and the attributes that differentiate you from your competitors. Also, maintain consistency of your brand across all channels to help your audience recognize your brand and build brand loyalty.

3. **Have an online presence.** Any business that is not online in this digital age is missing out on potential clients. These days, when people are searching for a service, the first thing they do is check on Google. Will they find you if they search for your business on Google? This is a question you must ask and answer. Build a website and have it professionally designed, user-friendly, and optimized for search engines (SEO). This will help your website show up when people search for services in your niche. Constantly update your website with recent changes and services, maintaining high-quality and relevant content that adds value to your website visitors. Build your Google Business profile and list your business in online directories in your industry. If you are just starting your business, a website may not be among the first things you do because of the cost of creating a high-quality website, but as you grow, know when to invest in one.

4. **Invest in content marketing.** This involves creating and sharing high-quality content to attract and retain customers. Content marketing can be done through podcasts, blog posts, infographics, and more. To achieve results with this strategy, your content must be engaging, informative, and helpful to your audience. The message must be delivered in a way that appeals to your audience. Be creative and mix different styles to see what works for your brand while maintaining your brand voice.

5. **Leverage social media.** Social media is powerful! People are closing deals worth millions of dollars every day on social media platforms,

while others are using them just to find the latest gossip or waste time. What about you—are you leveraging social media to promote your business? If you haven't already, identify the social media platforms your target audiences use the most and create your accounts. Then, begin to actively engage on those platforms by creating regular posts, sharing relevant content, and participating in conversations. Social media is one platform where you can market and promote your business for free or at a reduced cost. You pay nothing to make posts that millions of people can see. A 2023 Statista report showed that 4.95 billion people are on social media, which is 61.9% of the world's population. Social media has huge potential for every business. However, you must consistently post relevant content that will attract and keep people glued to your page. Here are some tips to help you succeed in promoting your brand on social media:

- There are several major social media platforms, and you don't need to be on all of them, although it is recommended to maximize all platforms. Find the platforms where your audience spends their time and choose that platform to concentrate most of your social media growth effort. For example, LinkedIn is a great platform to connect with professionals and B2B companies, while TikTok or Instagram are better for businesses interested in attracting younger consumers. You need to understand your audience demographics and then conduct research to find where they spend their time.

- Have a consistent brand voice and personality across all social media channels. If your brand personality is a playful or youthful one, maintain that voice and style, whether posting on TikTok or LinkedIn. This consistency helps to build brand recognition and loyalty. Let your voice and style reflect in your posts, interactions and replies across all platforms.

- Share high-quality content. Don't post just because you are told to be consistent in your posting. Ensure the content you share is valuable, relevant, and engaging to your audience. Research the type of content your audience would like to see, and take the time to create such content. Use well-written and edited text, high-quality images, and engaging videos. Try different types of content, from entertaining to educational, to keep your audience engaged.

- Engage with your audience. As you become consistent on social media, you will begin to receive comments, messages, and mentions. Do not ignore these. Respond to your comments and messages, and, most importantly, respond on time. Engage in conversations both on your own page and on other similar pages so people see that there are real people behind your brand. As they see you constantly engaging your audience, you will build trust and loyalty in your brand.

- Leverage paid advertising. Consider investing in social media advertising to grow your reach and increase engagement. Platforms like Instagram, Facebook, and even LinkedIn offer various targeted advertising plans that can help you reach either a specific audience or a broad one. Facebook and Instagram particularly have tools where you select the location of your audience, their demographics, and other factors that will ensure your promotion gets to the right people. While you may not have the funds to run paid promotions often, utilize them for important events, discounts, and sales to create awareness of your brand.

- Post regularly and at the times when your audience is likely to be online. When you start growing your social media presence, it will help to post every day. Some businesses do as many as three posts daily. What is most important is to maintain a consistent posting schedule to keep your audience engaged and informed. There are several analytic tools you can use to know the best times to post; this is the time when your audience is online and most active. Also, you can schedule posts in advance on Meta Business Suite for both Instagram and Facebook, and the software will suggest times when your audience is most active.

- Leverage hashtags. Hashtags are a type of metadata tag that people use to make their posts more discoverable and have a wider reach. Hashtags help to increase the visibility of your posts.

However, you must ensure you are using the right hashtags for your content. Don't just stuff in hashtags for the sake of having them. Make sure they are relevant and right for the content you are putting out. Along with using popular hashtags, you can also create your own unique hashtags for brand recognition and to foster your own community.

- Collaborate and partner with influencers. Social media influencers are people who have successfully grown their following on social media because of their popularity, expertise, or reputation in their industry or niche. They can often influence the opinions, behaviors, and purchasing decisions of their followers. They can help you reach a larger or more focused audience. Look for influencers with an engaged audience whose values align with your brand values, and collaborate with them to share your brand. Remember that it is not just about the number of their followers but also the percentage of followers that engage with their content, as some people purchase fake followers. If an "influencer" has a lot of followers but little engagement, they may not be right for you.

- Monitor your social media data and adjust your strategy accordingly. On every social media platform, you can find data showing your page performance, the engagement rate and the number of people following or interacting with your page. Look for terms such as follower growth rate, engagement rate, and click-through rate. These metrics show the effectiveness of your social media strategy. Review this data regularly to see what works and what doesn't. Look at posts that did well and replicate them.

- Host contests and giveaways. This is one great way businesses increase their engagement and reach on social media. They encourage people to share, tag and comment to stand a chance to win a defined prize. This way, they leverage the contact of their followers to reach more people. When using this strategy, gift something that will appeal to your target audience to get better results. Usually the prize is a free or discounted product or service.

- Offer exclusive deals to your social media followers. This strategy will reward your current followers and encourage others to follow your profile.

- Share customer success stories and testimonials to build trust. Your audience wants to read and hear from people who have used your product or service to help their decision-making. Sharing these stories and testimonials on social media will attract potential customers while showing appreciation to the reviewer.

- Utilize live video. All the social media platforms, including Facebook and Instagram, have a live video feature that allows you to go live in real time and engage with your audience. This is a great way to add a personal touch to your social media presence. It's also an opportunity for you to speak with your audience and answer any questions they may have.

- Develop a social media content calendar. This calendar lists what content you intend to put out for each day of the week. It helps organize your content and helps you post consistently. It also enables you to schedule posts well in advance so you don't spend so much time posting every day.

- Keep up with social media trends. Be among the first to explore new platforms, as that gives you the first-mover advantage. Things change fast on social media. Stay current and be willing to adapt your strategy to enjoy new features and trends.

Remember that growing your presence on social media will not happen overnight. You will need to apply patience, perseverance, and a willingness to adapt your strategies to new trends. The more you show up on social media, the more you can enjoy the rewards of the platform. Keep going, whether you see results or not. People are watching to gauge your consistency. They will follow you once they trust your brand.

6. **Email marketing.** Email marketing is another great tool for promoting your business. This strategy involves building an email list and

sending regular newsletters, personalized content, and promotional offers to your subscribers. It is a direct way of communicating with your audience, clients, and potential clients. You can use it to promote your business, share updates, and build a community. You must ensure your emails offer value so that readers won't mark them as spam or, worse still, unsubscribe from your list. Let's look at some ways you can build your email list.

- Create high-value content and offer it for free on your website, then encourage visitors to subscribe to your mailing list to have useful content like the one they are reading delivered straight to their inbox.

- Create something of high value and offer it to your audience in exchange for their email address. This is what is known as a lead magnet. Lead magnets entice readers with something of great value in exchange for their email. It could be an eBook, a discount code, a free trial, a webinar, or other resources that are valuable to your target audience. Before using this strategy, research ideas for your offer and make it appealing and enticing.

- Have a direct email sign-up on your website, particularly on the page that is most frequently visited (you can find this data through Google Analytics or any other performance tools you may be using). This signup form could be in the header, footer, or sidebar. It could also appear as a pop-up. Make sure the sign-up process isn't lengthy and confusing, or else you risk losing your audience.

- Ask your social media followers to sign up for your email list. But before you do this, share exclusive offers available only to email subscribers or share snippets of your newsletter content. Whatever you share must be interesting enough for your followers to want to share their email addresses with you.

- Run online contests and giveaways and require participants to sign up with their email address to enter the contest. Again, make sure the prize is right for the participants to attract quality sign-ups.

- Create special offers for your email subscribers, such as insider information or early access to events or services. This will motivate others to join your email list.

- Host online workshops or webinars to teach something of interest in your area of expertise. Require email sign-up as part of the registration process.

- If you have a physical office, you can have sign-up sheets in-store to collect email addresses. You can also include your sign-up link on your business cards or brochures with a call to action to join your email list.

- Partner with other businesses to promote each other's email lists. This is becoming a very common option on social media. Businesses are reaching out to seek this collaboration. Look for groups with complementary businesses and collaborate. This will help you reach a new but relevant audience.

- Use paid advertising on search engines or social media to promote your lead magnets, directing visitors to the landing page where they can find and sign up for your email list.

- If you have an e-commerce store, add an option for shoppers to subscribe to your email list on the checkout page.

- Create a blog, post useful and engaging content, and then end each post with a call to action for readers to subscribe to your email list for more updates.

- Include a sign-up call to action in your email signature. This is a soft way to encourage people you are communicating with to join your email list.

Remember that it is not about how many subscribers you have but the quality of the subscribers. You don't want to have people who are not engaged or interested in your offerings. It is better to have a small list of interested and engaged subscribers than to have a large list of people who never open your emails. Let your message be clear so that only the right audience will subscribe. Also, always respect people's privacy and comply with data privacy laws. In the US, these include the Privacy Act of 1974, the Health Insurance Portability and Accountability Act of 1996 (HIPAA), and the Children's Online Privacy Protection Act of 1998 (COPPA).

7. **Build and grow a solid network for your business.** Join local business groups and CEO roundtables, attend industry events, and engage in community activities. Here you can meet new people and share your business with them. This is also a great opportunity for people to place a face on your business, which will help increase brand loyalty and trust.

8. **Reviews.** Encourage happy customers to leave reviews on your social media pages, your Google Business page, and your website. Positive reviews are a great way to promote your business to new clients who may be doubting your legitimacy. It helps to increase your business credibility and attract new customers.

9. **Offer discounts and promotions.** Studies have shown that many people will readily switch brands if the other brand is offering a service at a lower price and the same quality. So if you want to attract new customers and retain existing ones, have periodic promotions and discounts. Think about how you started patronizing a brand: was it a limited-time discount, a loyalty program, or a bundle deal? All these programs encourage new and existing customers to buy from you.

10. **Invest in paid advertising.** No matter how big or small your business may be, have an assigned budget for paid advertising to increase your visibility significantly. Start with a small budget, test different ad campaigns, and increase your budget as you begin to see success. You may also consult with an ad specialist for better results with your ad investment.

11. **Participate in and host events.** Attend expos, trade shows, and conferences relevant to your industry. There are always events going on in every industry. Stay abreast of all these events and attend the ones that work for you. Also, consider hosting your own workshops, seminars, or conferences to showcase your expertise and connect with your potential

customers. It is never too early for you to host your own event. The turnout may not be so great at the start, but stay consistent, and one day the result will be good.

12. **Utilize the power of public relations (PR).** Public relations is about managing your brand's reputation and increasing brand visibility through media coverage. Write press releases about your events, achievements, or product launches and distribute them to local newspapers, online news sites, industry publications, and magazines. Press releases are not just for the big guys. Anyone can use them to grow brand awareness and manage their reputation.

13. **Create referral programs.** Particularly for new and growing businesses, one of the fastest ways to get new clients is through word-of-mouth referrals. You get more results when people are out there advocating for your brand. Create a referral program that rewards customers for referring new clients to your business. Through this, existing customers will be motivated to promote your business, and you will enjoy new customers. You can send out a survey to your existing customers to learn what rewards they would like in exchange for their referrals, then use their feedback to create your referral program.

14. **Analyze promotional strategy.** Last, as you promote your business, remember to analyze the effectiveness of whatever promotional strategy you may be using. Tools like social media analytics to gauge engagement, Google Analytics to track website traffic, and customer feedback to understand their perception of your brand are very crucial for your business. Use the results from the analysis to make any necessary adjustments to grow your brand.

To promote your brand effectively and successfully, you have to be creative and have tested strategies. Understand your audience, build a powerful brand, leverage all the marketing tools available, and analyze your effort to achieve results and drive growth. Remember that it is not enough to reach a wide audience; you need to engage them in meaningful ways to create lasting relationships with them.

Here are some powerful affirmations to inspire you as you commit to engaging your audience and promoting your brand. Use them as a daily reminder of your capabilities and potential in promoting your business. They can help reinforce a positive mindset and drive towards successful marketing endeavors.

★ I have the creativity and determination to effectively market my business.

★ Each promotion I create brings valuable customers closer to my brand.

★ I am confident in my ability to communicate the value of my products/services.

★ My marketing efforts resonate with my target audience and lead to success.

★ I am constantly attracting new opportunities to showcase my business.

★ With every step, I am becoming more skilled in promoting my business.

★ My strategies in marketing are innovative, effective, and impactful.

★ I am adept at turning challenges in promotion into growth opportunities.

★ Every marketing campaign I launch increases my visibility and influence.

★ I confidently navigate the landscape of business promotion with ease and expertise.

★ My promotional activities are a reflection of my passion for and commitment to my business.

★ I am a magnet for positive attention and recognition in my industry.

★ With each promotional effort, I am building a loyal and engaged customer base.

★ I am skilled in utilizing social media to expand my business's reach.

★ I create marketing content that is engaging, inspiring, and persuasive.

★ My promotional strategies are leading my business to new heights of success.

★ I am constantly learning and adapting to maximize my promotional impact.

★ I am an expert in identifying and capitalizing on marketing trends.

★ My business stands out in the market through innovative and effective promotion.

★ I am grateful for the growth and opportunities that my marketing efforts bring.

CHAPTER 6

Harvesting the Power of Relationships

Lesson No. 6:

Build meaningful relationships that will provide you with the right resources and support to excel in your life's journey.

Why is networking such a big deal? Because the world is about who you know. But networking goes deeper than just who you know. It's also about who knows you and what they think of you. You may know the right people, but if they don't think about you in the right capacity, they will never contact you to do a job.

Some people get their first client the first week of starting a business. For others, it may take as long as a month or even a year. I got my first client two weeks after leaving corporate America, and this happened at a networking event. My second client, too, came from a networking event. I am not sure if I would have gotten clients that early if I hadn't gone out and networked. Even people who get their first client in their first week by means other than networking probably enjoyed that success because of who they know and who knows them. We cannot go far in the business world or in any area of life without having the right network of support. Networking has been one key lifeline of my business. It has helped me over and over again to get and keep clients. Your network can open doors you didn't even know existed.

Through networking and events, I've gained clients, partnerships, and referrals and built meaningful relationships. These are connections I didn't have within my circle previously.

To many people, networking is about exchanging business cards and talking about what you do right on the spot. However, I like to see networking as building genuine, meaningful connections with others. And, although it may take some getting used to, networking can really be rewarding and fun.

How to Network

Even though we keep reading about networking, we sometimes don't have the tools and knowledge to network the right way. So, here are some practical networking tips that will help you navigate and make the most of your connections:

1. The first thing is to understand the purpose of networking. A lot of us approach networking from the point of exchanging business cards. Both physical business cards and digital ones like HiHello and Blinq are great ways to pass on your business information, but networking is about more than just exchanging contact information. It's about building relationships by taking the time to learn about the other person and their interests, likes, experiences, and views. So, when next you go to a networking event, go ahead and offer your card, but also show genuine interest in wanting to know about the other person. Ask about their interests, successes, and challenges. When you approach networking with the right mindset of building genuine relationships rather than just selling something from the start, you set the stage for more meaningful and productive interactions.

2. Before you go to that networking event, do your homework. Understand the nature of the event and its purpose. Know who is going to be there, and be clear about what you want to achieve. This preparation will help you target your efforts more effectively, enabling you to connect with the right people and engage in meaningful conversations that align with your professional goals.

3. Remember how you prepared for class presentations at college? The same applies here. When you meet people for the first time, you need to describe who you are and what you do. Make sure you have a concise and interesting narrative to do this. This "elevator pitch" should be

short, not salesy, and engaging enough to get the other person interested in knowing more about you. If you do this well, you will probably spend the rest of the time building a relationship with the other person.

4. Be genuinely interested in learning about the other person, about who they are and what they do. People can tell when interest is not genuine. Make sure you are present in the conversation. Ask open-ended questions, listen actively, use the correct body language, and engage with what they are saying. This will help you not only build rapport but also understand how you may be able to help them or vice versa.

5. Don't limit networking to in-person events alone. Social media platforms and industry-specific forums present excellent networking opportunities. Facebook, for instance, has different groups to serve different audiences, like groups for business owners in a niche, groups for female or male business owners, groups for business owners in a specific city, and so on. The list is endless. LinkedIn has several ways you can connect with professionals in your business, and the same is true with other forums and social media platforms. Join conversations, engage with content relevant to your field, and, if you find someone you think you may learn from, don't be shy about contacting them with a thoughtful message or comment. Several people I know have found mentors through online networking.

6. While you are networking, connect people to each other. This is one of the most powerful things you can do in networking. If you know two people who could benefit from knowing one another, make the introduction. Apart from helping them, it will establish you as a resourceful and valuable contact. People will see you as someone who knows the right people and will always keep you at the top of their minds.

7. After you leave an event or after meeting someone, make it a habit to follow up. Whether via a phone call or a LinkedIn connection request, following up with new contacts will help solidify your relationship. Don't wait until you need something from them before reaching out. Remember to reference something specific from your conversation with them to show them you were genuinely interested. It could be talking about their personal lives or their thoughts concerning a business topic.

Ensure whatever you are referencing is of value to them, as that will make them appreciate you more.

8. Think about how you can add value to your contacts. People appreciate those who add value to their lives. You could share a helpful article, provide a solution to a problem they mentioned, or offer your expertise on a topic. As long as you add value to your relationships, you will enjoy a lasting professional connection with your contacts.

9. Be open to various networking events. Don't restrict yourself to only events in your industry. Your audience can be in any event. Broader networking events, workshops, seminars, and other community events can be just as valuable. Attending these events can lead to connections you may not have made otherwise.

10. If you don't feel comfortable walking up to people and striking up conversations, practice. Start with smaller, less intimidating events and slowly work your way up. As you practice, you become perfect. Networking is a skill, and just like all other skills, you need to practice it to perfect it.

11. Let your network know about your professional life. LinkedIn is very useful for this. On LinkedIn, people share every milestone not because they want to boast but because they need to keep their network updated. Share new ventures, changes in your career, successes, and any sort of good thing that is happening in your professional life, and sometimes bad things too. During the mass downsizing in the IT space, we saw how people who lost their jobs at big firms like Google got other job offers just by sharing how they were affected by the downsizing. Updating your professional activities helps to keep your network engaged and aware of your progress. It also places ideas in their minds on ways they could be a part of your progress.

12. Be patient. Don't be discouraged if your networking efforts don't convert instantly to sales. Good relationships take time to grow. It's just like planting a seed. You will need to constantly water it by providing value for it to grow healthy. You must be patient and persistent. Keep watering your relationships, and one day you will enjoy the result of your hard

work. Even people who don't patronize you directly will probably refer you to others who will benefit from your service whenever the opportunity arises.

13. Do not pretend to be something you are not. Be authentic; be yourself. People are drawn to genuine people. If someone doesn't like you because of your personality, then they are not right for you. Show up as your true self (in a good way), and you will find it easier to connect with like minds on a meaningful level.

14. As you meet more people and grow your network, it is important to have a system for managing your contacts. A simple spreadsheet or CRM software such as ZoHo can help you keep track of people you meet, important details about them, and the last time you reached out. Having such a system is important as it helps prevent contacting someone too often or too seldom. It also gives you something to refer to when talking with them. You'll know what they like and what you can talk about.

15. Volunteer your time. Volunteering is one of my favorite things to do. It's a great opportunity to connect with others. It shows you are willing to invest your time in a cause you believe in. It also shows you are genuinely interested in providing value to others. Volunteering is also an avenue to network in a more relaxed setting, making it easy for you to connect with others faster and better than in a large gathering.

16. Always be ready to network. In this day and age, opportunities to network can spring up from anywhere at any time, whether on a flight, in a line at the grocery store, or at a formal event. Always be prepared to introduce yourself professionally. Dress neatly at all times so you can maximize these opportunities when they come.

17. If you find it intimidating to walk into a room full of strangers, consider going to events with a networking buddy. This will help ease the pressure as you both walk around finding the right connections.

18. Have a clear, achievable networking goal for every networking event. It could be as simple as finding a potential mentor, meeting two new people

or even learning something new. Having a goal will help you stay focused and motivated. Remember to set clear and simple goals. Do not set yourself up for failure by setting unachievable goals, as that will affect your self-esteem and will not put you in the right mindset for other networking events.

19. Always look for ways to give back to your network. Networking is a two-way street; it requires both parties to contribute to the growth of the relationship, whether through mentorship, advice, or support. Giving back will ensure you add value to the relationship, thereby sustaining it.

20. As your business grows and evolves, so should your contacts. Don't stop looking out for new connections while you nurture your existing ones. Your business goals will always change as you meet and set new goals. You want to ensure that you have a dynamic and evolving network that aligns with where you are as a business and as an individual.

Overcoming Networking Fear

I do not want to pretend that networking is always easy. Although it comes naturally to some, it can be intimidating to others. You may genuinely feel a sense of fear and anxiety at the thought of mixing with others. The need to make an excellent first impression just heightens our fear and self-consciousness. But, like every other fear, you can address and overcome the fear of meeting new people so that you can shine and network to grow your business. Here are ways that have helped me overcome this fear:

1. The first thing is to acknowledge where this fear comes from. For me, I knew my fear was from the rejection I suffered as a child. I constantly did things to make people like me, yet I still felt I wasn't liked much, even by my family. So I didn't expect strangers to like me. For you, it may be a lack of confidence in your social skills or not knowing how to start a conversation. Knowing what is causing the fear is the first step towards overcoming it. When the root of a problem is found, it becomes easier to fix. Once you find the root cause, take steps to address it.

2. It's okay to start with smaller events. When you feel ready for in-person events, start with a coffee meet-up with a colleague or a small local gathering. Small events present less intimidating environments that will help build your confidence.

3. Before you go to any event, take time to prepare. Preparing ahead will help reduce anxiety. You could write down your introduction and read it back to yourself several times while looking in the mirror. Research has shown that speaking to yourself positively helps build self-confidence and self-love. Also, preparing conversation starters can help reduce anxiety as you bring up topics you are familiar with and have prepared for.

4. Get to the event early to allow you to settle down and calm your nerves before more people arrive.

5. The goal is quality and not quantity. It is better to have a few meaningful conversations than to try to talk to everyone in the room. You may speak to only one person, but if the conversation is so good that you both leave feeling enlightened, then you have done well. This approach will remove the pressure that comes with networking and allow you to focus on building genuine connections.

6. Create your elevator pitch ahead of time. This is a quick and concise way to introduce yourself and what you do. Rehearsing it ahead will build your confidence and prepare you for when someone asks, "What do you do?" This question comes up in every networking situation, so having your elevator pitch handy and rehearsed will help you present yourself more confidently.

7. Practice active listening. I have found that some people's way of coping with anxiety is to talk too much. Most people find this off-putting. Networking is about talking and listening. Consciously remind yourself to allow the other person to share things about themselves, and show genuine interest in whatever they say. Show them you are a good listener, and they will be excited to talk to you for the rest of the event.

8. Pay attention to your body language. Body language can either invite people or repel them. Sometimes you may be saying the right things, but your body is saying something else. Have you ever walked into a room full of people and approached someone because you sensed they were approachable? This was probably because they had positive body language. Having positive body language will make you appear more confident and approachable. Smile, maintain good eye contact, and face the person you are speaking with. These nonverbal cues are game changers in how others perceive you.

9. Find a colleague or a friend to attend events with. Sometimes, what makes networking seem intimidating is when we happen to be the only ones who don't know someone else in the room, so it often helps to go with someone you are familiar with. But remember that they are only there to support you. Don't get so comfortable talking with them that you forget to meet other people!

10. Leverage online networking events to build your confidence in interacting with others. If online networking is too intimidating, start with text-based online forums where no one sees you. Sign up for webinars, join relevant online groups, and send connection requests to others with similar interests. The digital world has now made it easy and possible to connect both online and offline. Feel free to ask questions respectfully, share your feedback and reach out via messages. Remember that in the online space, whatever you write will always be remembered, so make sure you are adding value to conversations and not creating controversies.

11. See every networking opportunity as a chance to learn about your strengths and weaknesses. After an event, reflect on the things you did well and the ones you could have done better. So you didn't sound too confident when introducing yourself to that contact. What would you do better next time? It is not a time to condemn yourself but rather to learn so that you can put what you've learned into practice at the next event.

12. Remember that everyone in that room is human, regardless of their position. They, too, have their awkward moments and will likely understand how you feel.

13. Set realistic expectations. You cannot become a networking guru overnight. You will make mistakes. You will go to events and hide, and that's okay. These things take time. If you make mistakes at one event, forgive yourself and try again at the next one. Start with small, realistic goals like introducing yourself to at least one person in the room or even staying for at least thirty minutes. Then, increase your expectations as you ace each one.

14. As soon as you grow your confidence in smaller settings, challenge yourself to attend larger events. Don't stay stuck on online or small group events. Challenging yourself and taking steps to pass the challenge will help build your confidence steadily.

15. As you meet people, shift your focus from what you can get from them to how you can help take pressure off them. Focus on how you can serve them and not how they can help you meet your sales goals for the month. When you approach networking from the perspective of assisting others to become better, it becomes less about personal performance and more about mutual benefit.

16. Remember to follow up after the event. Networking shouldn't end for you when the event is over. The same day or the day after, reach out to the new contact through a personalized text message, email, or LinkedIn message to help cement the relationship you've started.

17. Continue to show up no matter how the last event went. The more you show up and network, the more comfortable you will become. I find that the more I talk about myself and what I do, the more confident I become. I may have been timid when I started, but I can now address a room full of people with my head held high. It is all about consistency. See every event as an opportunity to practice and perfect your skills.

18. Consider seeking professional help if your fear of networking is deeply rooted. Workshops, groups, coaches, and therapists can help you reduce anxiety and improve your social skills. Some groups are specifically about helping people with public speaking and pitching their business. Seek help, and watch as your confidence is boosted.

19. Celebrate yourself every time you attend an event, start a conversation, or make a new connection. Celebrating these victories, no matter how little you may think of them, is vital in building confidence. Pat yourself on the back and say a big "Well done."

Remember that networking isn't just about adding contacts but building relationships with others. Approach it with the right attitude, and you will enjoy a world full of opportunities. Give yourself time to develop your networking skills. It will not happen overnight. Every successful person you see out there has had times when they felt like they weren't networking right. So take a deep breath and put your best foot forward. You've got this!

Here are some powerful affirmations for networking. Recite them before, during, and after every networking event to build your confidence:

★ I radiate confidence and charisma, drawing influential connections towards me.

★ Every conversation I engage in opens doors to new opportunities and collaborations.

★ I am a hub of ideas and opportunities, enriching every network I am part of.

★ I build genuine, lasting relationships that transcend professional benefits.

★ My networking skills are a catalyst for success, creating pathways for growth and innovation.

★ Networking comes naturally to me.

★ The idea of networking is something I genuinely love.

★ I am becoming a confident and well-connected individual.

★ I am important, and the prospect of connecting with other important people excites me.

★ I have so much to offer others, and my mere presence is a gift to my network.

★ I frequently encounter intriguing individuals.

★ I effortlessly forge powerful and positive connections with good people wherever I go.

★ I serve my network with respect, professionalism, and intelligence.

★ My network continues to grow exponentially every day.

★ I assist the people in my network in achieving their goals and objectives.

★ I effortlessly connect with new contacts and allies wherever I go.

★ I am a facilitator within my network, bringing people together for their mutual benefit.

★ I am a master at networking.

★ I thrive in large social settings, effortlessly connecting with both familiar and unfamiliar faces, building rapport, and deepening existing bonds.

★ I naturally attract brilliant co-creators.

CHAPTER 7

Cultivating Your Self-Care Garden

LESSON NO. 7:

Prioritize your well-being as you conduct your business. This means setting aside time for rest, engaging in activities that rejuvenate your spirit, nurturing your mental and physical health, and recognizing the signs of burnout. Just like a successful business, a balanced life is built on the foundation of self-care.

In all your getting, get rest. This is one of the key lessons I have learned on my journey so far. No matter how much time and effort you put into growing your business, if you do not take care of yourself, your business will not last. If you get burned out, you will lack the strength and motivation to push your business to the next level.

While we pursue success, we often neglect the very engine that drives our ambition—our well-being. The truth is that the health of your business and your personal health are intrinsically linked. They rely on each other to do well. Neglecting your personal health will lead to diminishing returns in your business, no matter how hard you work.

I used to push myself to complete exhaustion, working twenty-six hours straight or putting my whole life on hold to meet deadlines. The first time I caught COVID, I felt like I'd been hit by a truck. Even though I felt horrible, I refused to let it keep me down. I would answer a business call as lively as I could, masking the pain all over my body, the chills and sweat from a fever, and all my other symptoms. After each call, virtual meeting, or deadline, my body succumbed, and I would pass out as if I'd just been beaten up in a fight and needed to take a break. It was horrible. I could have healed from COVID quicker had I taken time for self-care. I could have delegated responsibilities or put certain things on hold until I recovered. After I made a full recovery, I realized how important it is to take care of my health.

Society has taught us that self-care is selfish. Most of us grew up hearing that we always have to place everything and everyone above our needs. We are called selfish if we ask for a moment to catch our breath. I spent most of my childhood doing everything for everyone and nothing for myself until I couldn't give anymore because I was drained. I had to learn to create time for me. I had to do a lot of unlearning and relearning to get to the level I am at now. I have learned that self-care is not selfish; it is not a luxury, either. It is a necessity. It is the only way you can keep giving of yourself to your business and everyone around you.

So in this chapter, let's explore practical self-care strategies for integrating wellness into the very fabric of your daily routine. From setting healthy boundaries to prevent burnout to cultivating habits that nourish both mind and body, we will delve into how to take care of yourself. After all, the true measure of success is not just in the wealth you accumulate but also in the quality of life you maintain while achieving those milestones.

Self-care is not just about your physical health but also about nurturing your mental, emotional, social, and even spiritual well-being. We will look at each of these aspects of self-care and explore practical tips to enjoy overall wellness.

Physical Self-Care

Physical self-care is about improving your overall quality of life, including your personal and professional lives. These are practices and activities that improve your physical well-being. We all know how busy life can be, but if you prioritize your physical well-being, you will notice significant differences in your mood, productivity, and long-term health. So, here are some practical strategies you can implement in your self-care routine to enjoy all the benefits of physical self-care:

1. Engage in regular physical activity. Studies have shown the numerous health benefits associated with exercise, including stronger muscles, better sleep quality, reduced risk of diseases, enhanced mental health, and improved cardiovascular health. Your body loses so much if you fail to exercise often.

   - Have a consistent exercise routine. The goal is to exercise for at least thirty minutes most days of the week. You can start with moderate exercise and add in more intense ones as you progress. It could be brisk walking, swimming, jogging, running, cycling, or any other form of cardiovascular exercise. Stick to a consistent routine to train your body to adjust quickly and begin to benefit from the rewards. My daily exercise routine includes yoga, taking my dog on twenty- or thirty-minute walks, and taking the stairs instead of the elevator.

   - Add in strength training exercises at least twice a week to build and maintain your muscle mass. As we age, we lose muscle mass, which impacts our health and daily functioning. Loss of muscle mass can cause reduced strength and mobility, among other issues. Strength training exercises will help you avoid these issues. Use resistance bands, weights, or bodyweight exercises like squats and push-ups to build and maintain your muscle mass.

   - Stay active throughout the day. A lot of our jobs these days require us to stay in one position for a long time. Take short breaks every hour to stand, walk, or stretch. You may also consider using a standing desk or an under-desk bike to stay active as you work.

2. Eat a balanced and nutritious diet. The foods you eat play a huge role in your physical health. Eating a balanced diet ensures your body gets all the energy and nutrients it needs to function optimally.

   - Eat a variety of foods, including fruits, vegetables, whole grains, lean proteins, and healthy fats. This will ensure your body gets all the nutrients it needs.

   - Drink plenty of water throughout the day to avoid dehydration. The National Academy of Medicine suggests about 3.7 liters of water for men and 2.7 liters for women. If you find it hard to drink, you can consider getting one of those customized water bottles with inspiration and times of day marked on them. This way, you know how much water you are drinking per hour. Remember that dehydration can cause headaches, fatigue, and decreased concentration.

- Limit your intake of processed and high-sugar foods and drinks. These foods and drinks can cause energy crashes and are not beneficial for long-term health.

3. Practice mindful eating. Mindful eating involves being present and focused on your eating and drinking, both inside and outside the body.

- Eat without distractions. Try as much as possible not to work or watch TV while eating. Pay attention to your meal; enjoy every bite.

- Listen to your body to know when to eat and when to stop eating. Your body signals you to let you know you are hungry or full. Learn to tell the difference between real hunger and stress eating.

4. Sleep well. While you sleep, your body uses the time to repair, regenerate and recover. The goal here is quality sleep and not just lying down. You might consider getting a smartwatch to help you track your sleep quality. I set my iWatch to notify me when it's close to my desired bedtime. My phone automatically goes into "sleep" mode so I won't be disturbed by any notifications while I rest.

- Establish a sleep routine and stick to it. Go to bed and wake up at the same time every day—seven days a week, if possible. This will help create a sleep–wake cycle for your body.

- Ensure you have a restful environment to help you sleep easily. A dark, cool, and quiet environment is most conducive. Consider using eye shades, earplugs, or white noise machines if needed.

- Reduce screen time before bed. Research has shown that the blue light emitted by screens can impact your ability to fall asleep. So it is recommended that you turn off electronic devices at least one hour before bedtime.

5. Go for regular health check-ups. Early detection of a health issue allows for timely treatment and can prevent a more serious health problem from developing. Work can wait.

- Schedule annual check-ups with your healthcare provider even if you feel healthy. Some health issues don't come with symptoms.

- Monitor your health and record any changes you experience, such as changes in weight, persistent pains, or unusual fatigue, and discuss them with your doctors to help them provide you with the right support and treatment.

6. Manage your stress levels before you become burned out. Chronic stress can cause big health problems, including hypertension, heart disease, and a weakened immune system.

- Incorporate relaxation techniques like meditation, deep breathing, or yoga into your daily fitness routine.

- Create time to engage in activities that you love and that help you relax, whether it is gardening, reading, window shopping, or painting. These leisure activities can provide you with a much-needed break from work.

7. Incorporate healthy workplace practices to support your and your colleagues' physical health.

- Use ergonomic chairs and keyboards. If possible, use standing desks. Let your workspace promote good posture for your back health.

- Take a break every hour to stretch, stand, and walk around. This will help boost blood circulation and reduce muscle strain.

8. Limit alcohol consumption and avoid smoking. Studies have shown that alcohol and tobacco present several negative impacts on one's health.

- If you drink alcohol, drink in moderation as consuming too much can cause health problems like increased blood pressure and liver disease.

- Seek help to stop smoking if you currently smoke, as smoking increases the risk of numerous diseases.

9. Where possible, incorporate more physical activities into your transportation.

- Walk or bike to your destination rather than driving.

- Use the stairs rather than the elevator.

10. Do exercises like yoga or tai chi to improve your balance, flexibility, and strength.

When you take care of your physical health, you set a foundation for all-round success in your life and your business.

Mental and Emotional Self-Care

Taking care of your mental and emotional health helps you manage stress, weather emotional ups and downs, and maintain mental clarity so you can make decisions more effectively. Here are some ways to incorporate mental and emotional self-care practices into your daily routine to foster your mental and emotional wellness:

1. Practice mindfulness and meditation. These are powerful tools for reducing stress and calming your mind. They help you focus on the present moment, thereby improving concentration, reducing anxiety and enhancing your overall emotional well-being.

- Schedule a few minutes in your day to meditate. You can use guided meditation apps like Headspace, Unplug, Buddhify, or Calm to get started and into the habit. YouTube is my preferred app for guided meditation.

- Practice mindfulness in your daily activities. Be aware of your environment, feelings, and senses without judgment. This is an opportunity for you to check in and see how you are feeling at that moment.

2. Physical fitness benefits your mind as well as your body. When you exercise, your body releases endorphins, which are natural mood lifters and can help reduce feelings of depression and anxiety.

   - Find a physical activity you enjoy, whether it is dancing, jogging, hiking, running, or even yoga, and make it a part of your daily activities.

   - Be consistent. Aim for at least thirty minutes on most days if you cannot achieve this every day.

3. Sleep well. Lack of sleep will leave you feeling cranky and unable to perform at your best.

4. Eat balanced meals and eat regularly. Don't skip meals if possible. Aside from helping you be healthy in your body, eating right also impacts your brain and mood.

5. Journal your thoughts and feelings. Studies have shown that journaling is a therapeutic way to process your emotions and reduce stress. In some ways, it can be likened to speaking with a therapist.

   - Keep a journal and spend a few minutes each day writing freely about your feelings, thoughts, and experiences. Pour out your heart in this journal. This is a no-judgement zone where you can express how you feel. The inspiration behind my writing this book started from a journal entry.

   - Write the things you are grateful for in your journal to help you shift your focus from what is not working in your life to what is working. This will help improve your mood and put you in the right mindset to move forward.

6. Set healthy boundaries to protect your mental and emotional health.

- Say no to projects that would stretch you more than you are willing to go. It is totally okay to not take on every request or invitation.

- Prioritize your own needs as well. If a request is going to clash with your personal needs, turn it down. You need some time for yourself, away from work and other obligations.

- Protect your time. Avoid answering calls or text messages during the time you've set aside for self-care. Putting your phone on "Do Not Disturb" will help limit the number of distractions during those time periods.

7. Grow your relationships with others. Relationships offer support, increase your sense of belonging, and reduce feelings of loneliness.

- Keep in touch with your friends and family through any means that works for you, whether in person or virtually.

- Join groups or clubs with like-minded individuals to foster a sense of community and receive emotional support when needed.

8. Learn how to manage your stress effectively to avoid anxiety and depression. Use stress management techniques like deep breathing and listening to calming music to reduce your stress level.

9. Seek professional help if you have issues navigating mental and emotional challenges on your own.

- Therapists can provide you with tools and techniques for coping with anxiety, stress, or depression.

- Join a support group to share experiences and have a sense of belonging.

10. Engage in creative activities to express your emotions and reduce stress.

- Try new creative activities like painting, cooking, writing, or even putting a puzzle together. These activities can provide you with a mental break and a sense of achievement.

- Start and complete a DIY project. Pinterest is a good place to look for ideas. Working on a do-it-yourself project can be a great way to relax and unwind.

11. Find ways to incorporate fun and laughter into your day.

- Watch a comedy show or movie. Funny pet videos can also give you a good laugh.

- Do something fun, whether it is playing a game, going for a fun outing, or just being silly. Make time for light-heartedness. Laughter is like medicine; it cures sadness and sorrow.

12. Spend time in nature to calm your mind and body. This is called nature therapy.

- Do some outdoor activities like walking in a park, hiking, or just sitting in a garden. The feel of the wind on your face and body helps to relax your mind and calm you. I love spending time in nature when I am stressed. It does magic for me.

- You can also bring nature indoors, like having plants in your working space or living room, to enjoy the same soothing effect.

13. Practice mindful breathing exercises to help you relax and focus.

- Take deep, slow breaths to relax and calm your mind.

- Try different breathing techniques like pursed lip breathing, belly breathing, and equal breathing to help you relax.

14. Take breaks from social media and even your digital devices. Sometimes seeing what people claim to have achieved online can cause depression when it looks like we haven't done much. That feeling is a sign that it is time to go on a digital detox.

- Set a specific time of the day when you will disconnect from all your digital devices.

- Have a tech-free zone or times when you are away from all gadgets. It could be before bedtime or during meals.

Social Self-Care

No man is an island; we all need other people to thrive and do well. This is where social self-care comes in. No matter how busy your work life may get, you must commit to addressing your social self-care needs. Here are some practical ways to enhance your social self-care:

1. Create time for social connections. Social connections are not time-wasters if you are dealing with the right people.

    *   Schedule regular meetups just like you would do for your business meetings. It could be a monthly dinner or a weekly coffee date. Make these meetings a priority.

    *   Stay in touch with your loved ones, whether it is just a quick text or a phone call. Technology has given us so many resources that we have no excuse not to stay in touch.

2. Invest in building meaningful relationships.

    *   Seek quality over quantity. It is not about the number of people you have in your circle but the value they bring. Focus on nurturing deeper connections with a few people whom you can trust rather than having many superficial relationships with people who cannot support you when needed.

    *   When you are with someone, be present. Give them your full attention. Engage in the conversation and listen actively. Let them know you are there with them.

3. Join groups or clubs with people whose interests are similar to yours, whether it is a book club, a sports team, or anything else you love doing.

4. Participate in local community events, classes, or workshops to meet new people and build a sense of community.

5. Volunteer in your field, either online or in your community, as a way to give back and grow your social network.

- Look for opportunities to serve in local shelters, charities, or community centers.

- Find volunteering opportunities in your field of interest or passion. This way, you will find fulfillment while connecting with others.

6. Strike a good balance between physical and virtual interactions.

  - Limit how much time you spend on social media. While social media has its own advantages, it can also lead to feelings of inadequacy or isolation. Balance your online interactions with in-person connections.

  - Use technology wisely to connect with distant friends and family members. If your friends and family are nearby, create time for physical meetings.

7. Invest in networking and building professional relationships.

  - Attend networking meetings, seminars, or conferences to broaden your professional network.

  - Join professional associations to enjoy both social and business benefits.

8. Set healthy boundaries even as you socialize.

  - Decline invitations or requests if they don't align with your needs or schedules. Taking them on will lead to burnout and resentment.

  - Share your availability and need for personal time with others so they know to respect your boundaries.

9. Develop your communication skills. Actively listen to what others are saying, and show your understanding and interest.

  - Be open and honest in your conversation with others.

  - Share your thoughts and feelings in a respectful way to deepen your connections.

10. Cultivate empathy. Look at things from the other person's viewpoint.

Don't always be the right one in the room. Consider the other person's experiences, too, and use that awareness to improve communication.

11. Offer your support and understanding to friends and family going through tough times.

12. Create time for family.

    • Plan and execute family outings or activities. They don't have to be elaborate. Something as simple as a picnic or a weekly game night is perfect for strengthening bonds.

    • Eat your meals together, as this is an excellent time to connect and converse.

13. Reconnect with old friends from school, work, or other places. Rekindling old friendships can be incredibly rewarding.

    • Occasionally contact people you've lost touch with. Social media has now made it possible to find and reconnect with old friends.

    • Attend reunions to reconnect with old friends and lost contacts.

14. Embrace new social opportunities. Say yes to new activities that do not clash with other engagements or personal time. Be proactive in organizing outings or get-togethers. Don't wait for others to make the plan all the time.

15. Participate in community activities and projects like local festivals, neighborhood clean-ups, or town hall meetings. Support local businesses to feel a sense of community.

16. Learn how to resolve conflicts before they escalate. Address them calmly and directly. Seek mediation or counseling if you cannot resolve them on your own.

17. Recognize that not all social interactions will be right for you. Give yourself compassion. You cannot be there for every single event you are invited to. Don't feel bad about it.

Healthy social self-care routines are the ones filled with quality interactions that bring you joy, support, and a sense of belonging. Find some that work for you, and commit to them.

Spiritual Self-Care

Spiritual self-care means nurturing your spirit and connecting with something greater than yourself. A spiritual self-care routine can be any practice that provides a sense of peace, meaning, connection, and a deeper understanding of life and oneself. Here are some ways to enhance your spiritual self-care:

1. Spend time in nature, whether it is a hike in the woods, sitting by a body of water, or just walking in the park.

2. Take time to reflect on your feelings, thoughts, and experiences. Think about the meaning of life and the things that are important to you.

3. Read spiritual texts, poetry, or literature for inspiration. Reflect on the meaning of what you've read as well as how it resonates with your life.

4. Engage in yoga and other movement practices like tai chi that combine physical postures, meditation, and breathing exercises. These activities allow you time to reflect.

5. If you follow a religious tradition, pray regularly. Attend religious services or gatherings that align with your beliefs and values. For me, the first thing I do every morning when I wake is to pray to God. I thank Him for waking me up in the morning and blessing me with a new day. I ask Him to lead and guide me in the direction He would have me go. God is the real essence of my being. I pray, study my Bible, and worship God.

6. Volunteer your time and perform random acts of kindness to create a sense of goodwill and spiritual fulfillment. Don't do these acts just for the sake of ticking a box. Look for causes that resonate with you, and support them wholeheartedly.

7. Connect with a group or community of people who share your spiritual values or interests. Spend time together to study spiritual books or practices, and support each other on your spiritual journeys.

8. Seek a spiritual mentor or guide, like your clergyperson, to offer you guidance and wisdom on your spiritual journey.

9. Create time for solitude. You want to reflect on your spiritual journey, where you are, and what needs to be done. This is a time to connect with your inner self and understand your beliefs, values, and life's meaning.

10. Have your own personal rituals that have spiritual significance to you. It could be reciting affirmations in the morning, declaring God's words over your life, lighting a candle, or spending some time in worship.

11. Participate in spiritual retreats and workshops to gain new insights for your spiritual growth. Read spiritual books that will help you explore different aspects of your spirituality.

12. Regularly write down the things you are grateful for, and make it a daily habit to express your gratitude to people whom God has brought into your life. Your appreciation could be done verbally or through acts of appreciation.

13. Work on letting go of offenses and forgiving those who wronged you. Holding on to resentment and anger can hinder your spiritual growth. One of the big things I had to do in my spiritual journey was forgive my parents and everyone who hurt me in my childhood. I knew I needed to do this to be free and enjoy my relationship with God.

14. If you feel stuck or conflicted in your spiritual journey, consider speaking with a spiritual advisor or therapist to help you find your grounding.

Like the other types of self-care routines, spiritual self-care routines differ from person to person. Whatever routines you choose, make sure they help you develop a sense of meaning, peace, and connection in your life. Find a routine that works for you and incorporate it into your daily life.

Here are some affirmations to support you in your self-care journey. Use them to foster a sense of self-love, peace and resilience.

★   I am deserving of rest and rejuvenation.

★   My well-being is a top priority in my life.

★   I give myself permission to pause and recharge.

★   Every breath I take fills me with peace and calm.

★   I am worthy of love and joy in every moment.

★   I embrace my strengths and accept my weaknesses with kindness.

★   I am capable of overcoming any challenges that come my way.

★   My mind is a sanctuary of tranquility and positive thoughts.

★   I allow myself to grow and learn from my experiences.

★   I am surrounded by an aura of serenity and confidence.

★   I trust in my ability to navigate life's journey with grace.

★   I cherish the unique person that I am.

★   I honor my body with nourishing choices and self-care.

★   Every day, I grow stronger and more resilient.

★   I am connected to an endless source of inner strength.

★   I radiate positivity and attract good energy.

★ I am in harmony with the world around me.

★ My heart is open to giving and receiving love.

★ I am grateful for the abundance of blessings in my life.

★ I move through life with ease and grace, knowing I am fully supported.

Conclusion

As we come to the end of this book, I hope the lessons I shared have inspired and equipped you for each season of your life. My sincere wish is that as you reflect on the stories, tips, and insights shared throughout these chapters, you feel empowered to take the right steps for your life and destiny. I hope you've found the inspiration to move to your next season, do the right things the right way, and love yourself wholeheartedly.

God guides us through all times and seasons, and if we trust Him, we will find the direction we need to go. Life is God's gift to us, with the opportunity to create our stories in fear and boldness. Think of life as your canvas and you as the artist. You have the power to create what you want in your life. Your story is still unfolding, and you have so many pages waiting to be filled with your sketches and stories from your journey.

Love yourself, and only then will you teach others how to love you. Invest in your personal development and growth. Discover your life's goals, and remain committed to achieving those goals. Take steps, make mistakes, and learn from your mistakes. If you fall, don't stay down. Dust yourself off and go again. Keep going until you crush it. Don't give up. Morning is close when the night is the darkest. Trust that you have everything you need to succeed in your goals.

Life is not always picture-perfect, but that is the beauty of life: sometimes messy, sometimes beautiful. Regardless of how it plays, you must acknowledge your story and make the best of each moment. Be your biggest cheerleader and let your voice be the loudest as you cheer yourself on to victory.

My company's logo—two mirrored letter Bs that form a butterfly—is emblematic of my personal journey as well as my business. The mirrored letters represent our forward- and backward-facing customer services, in which we aim to connect client candidates with client companies for a mutually rewarding relationship. The two Bs are also a hidden tribute to my late sister, whose initials were BB. She encouraged and inspired me to be the best version of myself and to go after what I wanted in life. I aspire to be an inspiration to others as she was to me. The butterfly represents transformation and evolution. Not only do we aim to transform the workforce through professional and personal development, but we also want to encourage them to transform their own lives into something they can be proud of. The purple is a symbol of strength, power, transformation, and royalty. We have the power and strength to transform our lives and businesses into anything we want.

Now it's your time to create the life you want, armed with God's guidance and direction. This is your journey, your story. You are the author and the main character of your story. You've got this!

About the Author

Rachel Bickham, a Houston native, embodies the epitome of resilience and entrepreneurial spirit, having triumphed over challenges to establish herself as a successful businesswoman. Growing up in Ponchatoula, Louisiana, and Oakland, California, Rachel discovered her passion for construction while working on her inaugural project in Oakland. This experience laid the foundation for her venture, Bickham Services Unlimited LLC, where she currently serves as the CEO.

With over two decades of experience, Rachel has navigated and excelled in handling multimillion-dollar projects catering to government, corporate, and private sector clients. Her expertise spans construction and project management, complemented by her proficiency in talent acquisition. This unique skill set allows her to build high-performing teams and effectively manage her business operations.

Rachel's journey is marked by her tenacity and ambition, evident in her ability to overcome obstacles with a positive outlook. From being a teenage mother, she defied the odds, culminating in the attainment of an associate degree just before her son's high school graduation. Holding a bachelor's degree in business administration and a Construction Documents Technologist (CDT) certification, Rachel is also an alumna of the prestigious Goldman Sachs 10,000 Small Business program.

Actively engaged in community service, Rachel pays forward the support she once received from organizations like the Salvation Army and the Red Cross. Volunteering at non-profits, she participates in activities such as feeding the homeless and contributing to charitable events. Beyond her professional pursuits, Rachel is an avid traveler, social networker, and art enthusiast, committed to making a positive impact on society.

Rachel's achievements further underscore her standing as a trailblazer in her field. Graduating from the Turner School of Construction in 2020, she received nominations for the HMSDC "Supplier of the Year" and "Strategic Teaming" Awards in 2021. Her recognition in the Houston Innovation Awards in 2023 and features in HTX Magazine and Canvas Rebel Magazine solidify her status as a noteworthy figure in both the business and entrepreneurial realms.

She wrote this book to share her wealth of entrepreneurial experiences and support others in their journey. She hopes that the lessons in this book will provide you with clarity on your entrepreneurial journey.

Rachel Bickham, CDT | CEO
Bickham Services Unlimited, LLC
www.BickhamServicesUltd.com
Instagram: https://www.instagram.com/bickham_services/
Facebook: https://www.facebook.com/BickhamServicesUltd
LinkedIn: https://www.linkedin.com/company/
bickham-services-unlimited-llc/

About Bickham Services Unlimited, LLC

Bickham Services Unlimited, LLC specializes in offering personalized staffing solutions to both private and government clients by matching quality talent with suitable opportunities. We provide a range of top-quality placements, including temp-to-hire, temporary, long-term, and direct-hire positions. Our experienced recruiting team has successfully staffed professionals in various industries, such as Construction, Information Technology, Industrial, Administrative, and Human Services.

As a certified minority and Woman Owned Small Business, Bickham Services places great importance on our recruiting and matching processes, which have been instrumental in our ongoing success in providing high-quality staff quickly and efficiently. We have built a wide network of talented individuals from diverse backgrounds. This well-established diversity network allows us to identify and qualify the most exceptional candidates and attract them to the organizations we work with.

To ensure we find the best-qualified candidates, we implement a staffing and recruiting plan that aligns with the latest industry trends in technology, skill demands, and compensation. We also take into consideration environmental factors, organizational structure and culture, job responsibilities, and business objectives in our candidate selection. Our team of recruiters is experienced in the industries we serve and, therefore, understands the importance of having competent personnel from both risk management and operational standpoints.

Customer Value Proposition

For small, medium, and large businesses, as well as government agencies seeking top talents in their industry, our staffing and recruiting services offer the right solution. We provide pre-screened and vetted candidates, taking care of time-consuming tasks such as resume screening, coordinating individual interviews, conducting skills test assessments, posting job openings, and implementing other marketing tactics to attract talented individuals. By acting as an extension of your HR team, we free up your time to focus on essential business operations. Our team of recruiters is highly experienced in the industries we serve, giving us a deep understanding of the importance of having skilled and competent personnel. We prioritize both risk management and operational effectiveness.

Notes

Notes

Notes

Notes

Notes

Notes

Notes

Notes

Notes

Notes

www.ingramcontent.com/pod-product-compliance
Lightning Source LLC
Chambersburg PA
CBHW021649120626
46545CB00002B/776